TRIO
READING 3

The Intersection of
Vocabulary, Critical Thinking, & Reading

Kate Adams

OXFORD
UNIVERSITY PRESS

198 Madison Avenue
New York, NY 10016 USA

Great Clarendon Street, Oxford, OX2 6DP, United Kingdom

Oxford University Press is a department of the University of Oxford.
It furthers the University's objective of excellence in research, scholarship,
and education by publishing worldwide. Oxford is a registered trade
mark of Oxford University Press in the UK and in certain other countries

ISBN: 978 0 19 400406 0 STUDENT BOOK 3 WITH ONLINE PRACTICE PACK
ISBN: 978 0 19 400385 8 STUDENT BOOK 3 AS PACK COMPONENT
ISBN: 978 0 19 400388 9 ONLINE PRACTICE WEBSITE

Printed in China

This book is printed on paper from certified and well-managed sources

ACKNOWLEDGEMENTS

Cover Design: Yin Ling Wong

Illustrations by: Ben Hasler: 6, 10, 11, 32, 33, 36, 37, 58, 59, 82, 83, 108; Joe
Taylor: 20, 21, 24, 44, 45, 70, 71, 97, 100, 120; 5W Infographics: 62, 64, 103.

*The publishers would like to thank the following for their kind permission to reproduce
photographs*: lzf/Shutterstock, pg. 1 (woman running); Brownstock/Alamy
Stock Photo, pg. 1 (mother and child reading); 145/Tom Grill/Ocean/Corbis,
pg. 1 (erasing answer); John Muggenborg/Alamy Stock Photo, pg. 4 (white
bag); enciktat/Shutterstock, pg. 4 (flower); Marc Romanelli/Getty Images,
pg. 4 (sweaty man); Brownstock/Alamy Stock Photo, pg. 4 (mother and child
reading); Rainer Dittrich/Westend61/SuperStock, pg. 4 (airplane); Steve
Wisbauer/Getty Images, pg. 4 (measuring cup and spoons); lzf/Shutterstock,
pg. 5 (woman running); Ashley Cooper/Age Fotostock, pg. 5 (car exhaust);
Paul Gilham/Staff/Getty Images, pg. 5 (soccer goalie); Tetra Images/Tetra
Images/SuperStock, pg. 5 (graduate); Blend Images/Alamy Stock Photo, pg. 5
(woman in snow); OJO Images/OJO Images/SuperStock, pg. 5 (sick man); Mike
Kemp/Tetra Images/Corbis, pg. 5 (woman checking mail); eurekaimages.
com/Alamy Stock Photo, pg. 5 (café sign); MBI/Alamy Stock Photo, pg. 8
(classroom); Dmitry Naumov/Shutterstock/OUP, pg. 8 (park); Image Source/
Image Source/SuperStock, pg. 8 (cars); Maria Janicki/Alamy Stock Photo, pg. 8
(chocolate shop); Mark Mason/OUP, pg. 8 (laptop); Monkey Business Images/
Shutterstock, pg. 8 (student); Dennis MacDonald/OUP, pg. 8 (newspaper);
Alexander Raths/Shutterstock, pg. 8 (scientist); f4foto/Alamy Stock Photo, pg.
8 (sushi bar); Nick Stubbs/Shutterstock, pg. 10 (beach); Niloo/Shutterstock,
pg. 10 (magazines); enciktat/Shutterstock, pg. 10 (flower); Monkey Business
Images/Shutterstock, pg. 10 (student); Mark Mason/OUP, pg. 10 (laptop);
Dinodia Photos/Alamy Stock Photo, pg. 10 (old man); Mint Images Limited/
Alamy Stock Photo, pg. 14 (man using phone); Image Source/Getty Images,
pg. 14 (student raising hand); RF Corbis Value/Alamy Stock Photo, pg. 14
(student); 145/Tom Grill/Ocean/Corbis, pg. 14 (erasing answer); Jacob Lund/
Shutterstock, pg. 15 (woman working); Ermolaev Alexander/Shutterstock, pg.
15 (man studying); Westend61/Getty Images, pg. 15 (people waiting in line);
GaudiLab/Shutterstock, pg. 15 (woman reading); TOPIC PHOTO AGENCY
IN/Age Fotostock, pg. 19 (Korean students); ISSEI KATO/Reuters/Corbis,
pg. 19 (robot); Andrew Olney/Getty Images, pg. 19 (boys laughing); TOPIC
PHOTO AGENCY IN/Age Fotostock, pg. 27 (Korean students); ISSEI KATO/
Reuters/Corbis, pg. 36 (robot); Stefano Cavoretto/Alamy Stock Photo, pg. 36
(robotic vacuum); JENS BUETTNER/epa/Corbis, pg. 48 (Usain Bolt); Goodluz/
Shutterstock, pg. 57 (man working); Patrick Molnar/Corbis, pg. 57 (children);
Paula Solloway/Alamy Stock Photo, pg. 57 (deaf man and interpreter); amana
images inc./Alamy Stock Photo, pg. 71 (girl eating rice); Patrick Molnar/
Corbis, pg. 71 (children); Paula Solloway/Alamy Stock Photo, pg. 71 (lonely
boy); Iakov Filimonov/Shutterstock, pg. 71 (woman shopping); Don Troiani/
Corbis, pg. 74 (Louis-Philippe de Rigaud de Vaudreuil); OJO Images Ltd/Alamy
Stock Photo, pg. 74 (businessman); Alan Schein Photography/Corbis, pg. 86
(power lines); National Geographic Image Collection/Alamy Stock Photo,
pg. 86 (prosthetic arm); Paula Solloway/Alamy Stock Photo, pg. 89 (deaf man
and interpreter); Ingo Arndt/Minden Pictures/Corbis, pg. 95 (chimpanzee);
migstock/Alamy Stock Photo, pg. 95 (cereals); Jonathan Griffith/Getty Images,
pg. 95 (avalanche); NetPhotos/Alamy Stock Photo, pg. 96 (Google search);
Ingo Arndt/Minden Pictures/Corbis, pg. 97 (chimpanzee); Chuck Pefley/
Alamy Stock Photo, pg. 109 (woman at supermarket); migstock/Alamy Stock
Photo, pg. 112 (cereals); Richard Levine/Demotix/Corbis, pg. 112 (jams) Kevin
Schafer/Alamy Stock Photo, pg. 121 (layers of rock); Wolfgang Weinhäupl/
Mauritius/SuperStock, pg. 121 (snowed in car); JIM EDDS/SCIENCE PHOTO
LIBRARY, pg. 121 (hurricane); StockShot/Alamy Stock Photo, pg. 121
(avalanche); Jonathan Griffith/Getty Images, pg. 124 (avalanche); tony french/
Alamy Stock Photo, pg. 124 (skier with airbags); Nadezhda1906/Shutterstock,
pg. 126 (Sky Park); Andrew F. Kazmierski/Shutterstock, pg. 127 (High Line
Park).

REVIEWERS

We would like to acknowledge the following individuals for their input during the development of the series:

Mahmoud Al-Salah
University of Dammam
Saudi Arabia

Robert J. Ashcroft
Tokai University
Japan

Karen E. Caldwell
Bahrain Polytechnic
Bahrain

Stephanie da Costa Mello
Glendale Community College
U.S.A.

Travis Cote
Tamagawa University
Japan

Ian Daniels
Smart ELT
Japan

Gail Fernandez
Bergen Community College
U.S.A.

Theresa Garcia de Quevedo
Geos Boston English Language School
U.S.A.

Patricia Ishill
Union County College
U.S.A.

Ji Hoon Kim
Independence English Institute
South Korea

Masakazu Kimura
Katoh Gakuen Gyoshu High School/
Nihon University
Japan

Georgios-Vlasios Kormpas
Al Yamamah University/SILC
Saudi Arabia

Ji-seon Lee
Jeong English Campus
South Korea

Sang-lee Lee
Kangleong Community Language
Center
South Korea

Zee Eun Lim
Reader's Mate
South Korea

James MacDonald
Aspire Language Academy
Kaohsiung City

Chaker Ali Mhamdi
Al Buraimi University College
Oman

Elizabeth R. Neblett
Union County College
U.S.A.

John Peloghitis
Tokai University
Japan

Whitney Tullos
Intrax
U.S.A.

Pingtang Yen
Eden Institute
Taichung City

Author Acknowledgments

A special thanks to my mentor in Teaching English as a Second Language at Northeastern Illinois University, Dr. Teddy Bofman, who counseled me that education is never over. A thank you to my students at the Illinois Institute of Technology for sharing their opinions, thoughts, and pursuits with me and to the community of faculty and friends I've met along the way.

Many thanks to Eliza Jensen for her discerning eye and diligent work on *Trio Reading* and to Anna Norris for sharing her enthusiasm and opinions in developing this series. Both were valuable collaborators.

And a thank you to my husband and son, my lifelong learning partners.

—Kate Adams

CONTENTS

Welcome to Trio Reading

Building Better Readers . . . From the Beginning

Trio Reading includes three levels of Student Books, Online Practice, and Teacher Support.

Level 1/CEFR A1

Level 2/CEFR A2

Level 3/CEFR B1

Essential Digital Content

iTools USB with Classroom Resources

Trio Reading's contextualized vocabulary instruction, accessible paired readings, and critical thinking activities provide students with the tools they need for successful academic reading at the earliest stages of language acquisition.

Vocabulary Based On the Oxford 2000 🔑 Keywords

Trio Reading's vocabulary is based on the 2,000 most important and useful words to learn at the early stages of language learning, making content approachable for low-level learners.

Making Connections for Critical Thinking

Make Connections sections encourage the development of critical thinking skills by asking learners to draw connections between themselves, texts, and the world around them.

Readiness Unit

For added flexibility, each level of **Trio Reading** begins with an optional Readiness Unit to provide fundamental English tools for beginning students.

INSIDE EACH CHAPTER

▲ BEFORE READING

Theme-based chapters set a context for learning.

Essential, explicit skills help beginning learners to gain confidence with academic reading texts.

CHAPTER **5** How Do We Fit In?
- Spelling patterns for the different sounds of *t* and *t* with other letters
- Understand phrasal verbs
- Make inferences
- Present, present progressive, and present perfect

▲ BEFORE READING ► Oxford 2000 ♪ words to talk about how we fit into society

Learn Vocabulary

A. Match each picture to the correct description.

_____ A **tradition** is something that people in a specific place have done or believed for a long time.

It's a tradition to drink tea in the afternoon in England.

__1__ Your **values** are your thoughts about what is wrong and right.

I share many of the same values as my parents about money. We save our money.

_____ **Society** is a large group of people who live in the same area and have the same ideas about how to live.

In many societies, children begin school around age five.

_____ To **fit in** is to be able to live in an easy and natural way with other people.

I fit in with my brother's friends. They like playing soccer too.

1.

2.

3.

4.

B. Match each sentence to the correct picture.

1. A popular **fashion trend** is to wear jeans.
2. It's **human nature** to laugh when others do.
3. In my **culture**, everyone learns to eat with chopsticks.
4. I feel **lonely** at my new school.

> **Oxford 2000 ♪**
>
> Use the Oxford 2000 list on page 133 to find more words to describe the pictures on these pages. Share your words with a partner.

C. When you **follow** someone or something, you do what someone or something says you should do. Write each collocation under the correct picture.

follow a fashion trend   follow directions   follow traffic signs

1. _____   2. _____   3. _____

GO ONLINE for more practice

Vocabulary is introduced in context and is built from the Oxford 2000 list of keywords.

Trio Reading Online Practice extends learning beyond the classroom, providing students with additional practice and support for each chapter's vocabulary, grammar, and skills instruction.

Sounds of English

Spelling Connection

🔊 A. Listen to the different sounds the *t* makes in the words below.

| fit | tradition | nature | clothing |

Notice the spelling pattern. Listen for /t/ in *fit*, the /ʃ/ in *tradition*, the /tʃ/ in *nature*, and the /ð/ in *clothing*. Note that *th* can also make the unvoiced /θ/ sound as in *think*. Use a dictionary to help you know when to use /ð/ or /θ/.

B. The following words are in the texts on pages 74 and 76–77. Write them in the correct column. Some words may belong in more than one column.

| action | architecture | particular | population | they |
| shirt | society | that | this | culture |

/t/ in *fit*	/ʃ/ in *tradition*	/tʃ/ in *nature*	/ð/ in *clothing*

Sounds of English boxes provide sound-symbol decoding practice and link fluency and reading skills to improve students' reading speed and comprehension.

▲▲ DURING READING

Accessible paired readings help students develop reading skills by offering more reading practice and the opportunity to make connections between texts.

Vocabulary Strategies and Reading Strategies are practiced with each reading, giving students the skills they need for successful reading.

▲▲ DURING READING ▸ Vocabulary strategy: Understand phrasal verbs
▸ Reading strategy: Make inferences

⊙ Reading 1

A. Use punctuation to help you read phrases. Give a short pause after a comma. Then go on to the next phrase. A period is used after a complete sentence or thought. Pause for a little longer between sentences. Listen to the text and focus on the pauses after commas and periods.

Why Is Fashion Important?

Stop and Think
What values does your fashion show?

By the 20th century, most people no longer wore handmade clothing. Fashion had changed. They dressed more simply and bought their clothes from stores.

Fashion is everywhere, in homes, in architecture, but especially in clothing. Ask yourself why you are wearing a particular color, length of pants, or design. Is it because you saw an advertisement or someone wearing something similar? Not everyone likes to say they **follow** fashion **trends**. However, it's **human nature** to want to **fit in**. Imagine walking into a room of people. Who do you talk to? Many people talk to the person wearing clothes like theirs. Some choose the person whose clothes they like. Whichever you choose, it is connected to human needs. The first and most important human needs are water and food, the things the body needs. The second most important are connected to feeling safe. The third is our deep need to **belong**. Fashion fits in with this need. Walk down the street and look at the clothes people wear. The clothes show who they are. They show the group the person connects with. Is it a businessman in a business suit or a student in a T-shirt and jeans? You can learn a lot about a person from his or her clothes. What do each of these people do? What do they value?

To try on clothes is to try on another identity, to be someone different. With our clothing, we tell the world about ourselves and the groups we identify with. Everyone follows fashion. Even if you don't follow fashion trends, what you choose to wear shows your **values**. What fashions are we following? Fashion is connected to **culture**. There are groups who have worn the same styles for hundreds of years. These people follow the **traditions** of the past. Other people try out new designs.

Often, developments in **society** change fashion. In the 18th century, wealthy men wore bright colors of silk and velvet. However, in the 20th century, they wore more standard, plain clothing. It was the fashion of business. Designers made these clothes so men could move and work easily. Fashion also is connected to society. As society changes, fashion changes too. For instance, most people no longer have their clothes individually made for them. Due to this, we all buy clothing from many of the same stores. This doesn't mean we don't have choices. Walk down the street of any big city and you'll see something new. But even if it's new, it fits in with a group or belief. That's why we choose to wear it. We want to be accepted in that group. We want to be seen as young, rich, or smart. Fashion will continue to change as society does. And what we wear will too because as humans we have a deep need to belong.

B. Read the

74 Unit 2 | Chapter 5

Check Your Understanding

C. Write *T* (true) or *F* (false). Rewrite false statements to be true.

1. ___F___ Following fashion is not connected to fitting in.
Following fashion is connected to fitting in.

2. _____ The need to belong is the most important human need.

3. _____ The clothes you wear show the group you belong to.

4. _____ Changes in society and business affect fashion.

Vocabulary Strategy

Understand Phrasal Verbs
Some verbs in English are phrases. They include a verb and a preposition.

verb preposition
It's human nature to want to **fit in.**

The meaning of the phrasal verb is different from the individual words. Most phrasal verbs can be replaced by another verb that means the same thing. *Fit in* means "belong."

Phrasal verbs are used often in English, so it's good to know their meanings. Follow these steps to help you.

1. Read the sentence and identify a verb + preposition. Note that not all verbs and prepositions are phrasal verbs. For example, in "I walked into the room," *walked into* is not a phrasal verb—*into the room* tells where the person walked.

2. Look for a verb + preposition that has a different meaning from the verb. Think of another verb that could be used in the phrasal verb's place.

GO ONLINE for more practice

D. Underline the phrasal verb in each sentence.

1. With our clothing, we tell the world about ourselves and the groups we <u>identify with</u>.
2. To try on clothes is to try on another identity, to be someone different.
3. Other people try out new things.
4. Can you figure out why fashion changes?

Reading Strategy

Make Inferences
Readers make inferences to help connect what they are reading to what they know. Making an inference can help you better understand the writer's ideas.

1. Read a sentence or group of sentences.
2. Think about why the writer included this information. What is the writer saying? What can you learn?
3. Make an inference to help you understand the writer's idea. Think of what you know and how it connects to the text.

Not everyone likes to say they follow fashion trends, but it's human nature to want to fit in.
Question: *Why don't people want to say they follow fashion trends?*
Inference: *I think the writer is saying that people like to be seen as different.*

GO ONLINE for more practice

E. Match each question to an inference based on the text on page 74.

Questions
1. __c__ Why do some people try out new designs?
2. _____ Why do people wear different clothes to different places?
3. _____ Why do people wear styles from the past?
4. _____ Why is trying on clothes like trying on a new identity?

Inferences
a. People want to be accepted where they go. They change their clothes so they fit in.
b. People look at your clothes and form an idea of what group you belong to. This might change your idea of yourself.
c. People want to show that they are creative and they like change.
d. People want to show they value traditions.

⊙ Reading 2

A. Read the text on your own.

What Is Culture Shock?

According to the United Nations Population Fund, in 2013, 232 million people, 3.2 percent of the world's population, lived outside their home country. In 2009, the United States and the United Kingdom were the most popular places to move to. However, people also leave these places. In 2013, the United Kingdom lost 400 citizens a day. Many of these people were college educated and looking for other job and social opportunities. There's a phrase for the effect making your home in another **society** and **culture** has on you: *culture shock*. A shock is a bad surprise, but that's not actually how most people experience culture shock. Culture shock is when someone feels he or she doesn't **belong** in a new country. First, most people feel excitement at being in a new place. There are opportunities and possibilities. However, the second stage is different. People now notice how the new place is different from home. Everyday things like ordering food in a restaurant, shopping, and using the train are different. These small things can seem big. People get upset. It's **human nature**. They compare their new place to home. They think of home as better. When you know how to do things, like communicate in the language, it's easier. At this point, many people feel **lonely**. And feeling lonely can affect how you communicate with others. Lonely people often see other people as a danger. They don't trust them. As a result, they don't talk to others. There are people all around them, but they feel that they don't belong.

A university website gives tips for people to **follow** to help with culture shock: (1) Do not think things will be like they are at home. How people do business and communicate and what times of day they eat are often different. (2) Talk to people. Show you want to learn about them and their culture. (3) Do not let one person's actions affect your idea of the whole society. (4) Understand that everyday things, such as how close people stand to one another, how people wait in line, and how long people pause in conversations, are different. For example, during conversations, most Americans do not let much time pass before they feel the need to start speaking. Other cultures are much more comfortable with pauses in conversation. People in different cultures have different **values**. Try to notice these things and understand the new culture you are in. You may want to connect with others from home. While it can be helpful to be with people from your country, try to identify with others. This doesn't mean you have to change who you are to **fit in**. Think about what you can share and what you can learn. If you concentrate on these things, then you can begin to feel less lonely. Maybe you are different, but you can feel different and also belong.

Stop and Think
What other differences are there between cultures?

Grammar in the Readings

Notice the present, present progressive, and present perfect in the readings.

Writers use present tense to talk about things that are true now.
*Fashion **is** everywhere, in homes, in architecture, but especially in clothing.*

Writers use the present progressive to describe something that is happening.
*Ask yourself why you **are wearing** a particular color, length of pants, or design.*

Writers use the present perfect to talk about something that happened in the past and is still happening.
*There are groups who **have worn** the same styles for hundreds of years.*

GO ONLINE for grammar practice

76 Unit 2 | Chapter 5

During Reading 77

Audio for each reading helps students make the link between spoken and written English.

Grammar in the Readings boxes highlight the most important language from the readings. Practice of each grammar point is provided as part of *Trio Reading* Online Practice.

AFTER READING

Summarizing and Retelling activities provide students with the opportunity to review the concepts and vocabulary learned throughout the chapter.

Three Make Connections sections in each chapter help students develop critical thinking skills by linking texts to their own lives, other texts, and the wider world.

Summarizing and Retelling

A. Complete the sentences with the words from the box. Some of the words have to be changed to fit the sentences. For example, *tradition* has to be changed to *traditions*. Then read the paragraphs to a partner to retell the ideas.

Adjectives	Nouns	Verbs
human	culture	belong
lonely	fashion	fit
	nature	follow
	society	
	~~tradition~~	
	trend	
	value	

1. Some things are part of _____. This means that everyone does or experiences these things. One of those things is the deep need to belong. We wear clothes to show the group we _____ in with. Sometimes people wear clothes to show they value _____ from the past. Other times people follow the newest _____ if they care about _____.

2. Many people experience _____ shock. This is when _____ is different from your home. Many people feel _____ in this situation. But there are tips you can _____. Understand that people have different _____. Focus on what you can learn about the culture. You may be different, but you still _____.

B. Use the words from the chart in Activity A to discuss the topics below with a partner.

1. Talk about a fashion trend. Why do you think it happened? Why do you think people follow it? Why do you like or not like it?

2. Talk about culture shock. How might people act when they have culture shock? What other tips could help them?

Word Partners

member of society
the rest of society
modern society
wider society
fit into society

GO ONLINE
to practice
word partners

Word Partners activities expand on vocabulary taught in the chapter so students acquire more high-frequency collocations.

◀◀ Make Connections: Text to World

A. Do you agree or disagree with the writers? Check the statements you agree with, and then discuss your ideas with a partner.

1. _____ The clothes you wear show who you are.
2. _____ Fashion is important to people because they want to belong to a group.
3. _____ No one's clothes are really different. They fit into an idea or group in society.
4. _____ Learning about a culture can help you feel better.
5. _____ You can be different and still fit in.

B. Think about the two texts. Complete the chart to make predictions.

Now	In the Year 2065 (Future)
1. People wear _____.	1. People will wear _____.
2. _____ is having an effect on fashion.	2. _____ will affect fashion.
3. In 2013, 3.2 percent of the world's population lived outside their home country.	3. In 2050, _____ percent of the world's population will live outside their home country.
4. Many people leave home to move to the United States or Great Britain.	4. People will leave home to move to _____ and _____.

C. Both texts discuss ideas that are connected to a person's identity. What other things affect how you think about yourself? Complete the web with your own ideas. Look at the Oxford 2000 keywords on page 133 and find five words to help you.

my connection to traditions in my culture

Identity. What affects my idea of myself?

Chant

GO ONLINE
for the
Chapter 5
Vocabulary &
Grammar Chant

Vocabulary and Grammar Chants found online help students internalize the target grammar structure and vocabulary for greater fluency when reading.

Trio Reading Online Practice: Essential Digital Content

Trio Reading Online Practice provides multiple opportunities for skills practice and acquisition—beyond the classroom and beyond the page.

Each unit of *Trio Reading* is accompanied by a variety of automatically graded activities. Students' progress is recorded, tracked, and fed back to the instructor.

Vocabulary and Grammar Chants help students internalize the target grammar structure and vocabulary for greater accuracy and fluency when reading.

Grammar Note 1 Present perfect to connect the present to the past
Complete the sentences with the present perfect form of the verb in parentheses.

1. The students _____ their notes and are ready for the test. (review)

2. If you _____ the book, then you will do well on the test. (read)

3. My sister _____ in Korea and she can speak a little Korean. (study)

4. _____ you _____ the test? The other students took it today. (take)

5. I _____ not _____ the research study. What does it show? (see)

6. We _____ not _____ to Japan, but we want to go in the future. (be)

7. Scientists _____ that learning involves many areas of the brain. (know)

8. I _____ not _____ to the news report so I can't answer your question. (listen)

[Try again] [Reset]   [Submit]

> Online Activities provide essential practice of Vocabulary, Grammar, and Reading and Vocabulary Strategies.

> Vocabulary and Grammar Chants provide further accuracy and fluency practice for every chapter.

Grammar in the Readings

Notice the present, present progressive, and present perfect in the readings.

Writers use present tense to talk about things that are true now.
Fashion is everywhere, in homes, in architecture, but especially in clothing.

Writers use the present progressive to describe something that is happening.
Ask yourself why you are wearing a particular color, length of pants, or design.

Writers use the present perfect to talk about something that happened in the past and is still happening.
There are groups who have worn the same styles for hundreds of years.

GO ONLINE for grammar practice

> GO ONLINE icons lead students to essential digital content.

---

my connection to traditions in my culture

Identity: What affects my idea of myself?

Chant
GO ONLINE for the Chapter 5 Vocabulary & Grammar Chant

Use the access code on the inside front cover to log in at **www.oxfordlearn.com/login**.

Readiness Unit

Words

Alphabetical order
Letter sounds in words
Rhyme
Word sounds, spellings, and meanings
Stressed and unstressed syllables

Parts of Speech

Nouns
Adjectives
Verbs
Verb tenses

Phrases, Sentences, and Paragraphs

Collocations
Sentences
Paragraphs
⬤ Make connections

UNIT WRAP UP ## Extend Your Skills

Alphabetical order

The order of the letters in the alphabet is called alphabetical order. Words in dictionaries are organized in alphabetical order.

A. Write each group of words in alphabetical order. Check your answers in a dictionary.

1. name napkin nap nature nail _____ nail name nap napkin nature _____

2. thank text ten tear time _____

3. mistake miss minute more many _____

4. enjoy energy English end equal _____

5. language last lead kite lost _____

Letter sounds in words

The sounds letters make can be different from the name of the letter.

> When does a vowel say its letter name? When there are two vowels or a vowel with *y*, say the name of the first vowel:
>
> t**ea**m   t**ea**   b**oa**t   m**ay**
>
> When there is a vowel-consonant-*e*, say the name of the first vowel. The *e* at the end does not have a sound:
>
> t**a**ke   l**i**ke   n**o**te   c**u**te   **a**ge

A. Look at the spelling patterns. Read the words in the box. Write them in the correct columns in the charts.

beach	clock	dad	face	float
kick	leg	lie	such	suit

Short Vowel Sounds				
short a /æ/	short e /ɛ/	short i /ɪ/	short o /ɑ/	short u /ʌ/

Long Vowel Sounds				
long a /eɪ/	long e /i/	long i /aɪ/	long o /oʊ/	long u /u/

B. Look at each vowel sound. Cross out the word that does not have the same vowel sound.

1. /ʊ/   a. pull   b. put   ~~c. fuel~~   d. full

2. /ɔɪ/   a. say   b. employ   c. enjoy   d. noise

3. /aʊ/   a. cloud   c. two   c. now   d. brown

C. The schwa sound /ə/ in a̲loud can be spelled by any vowel. Look at the words. Circle each vowel that makes the schwa sound. There may be more than one in each word.

1. notice   2. agree   3. contain   4. general   5. instrument

D. These vowel sounds have an /r/ sound. Match each word to a word with the same vowel sound.

1. /ər/ third ___c___

2. /ɪr/ fear _____

3. /ɛr/ air _____

4. /ɑr/ far _____

5. /ʊr/ sure _____

6. /ɔr/ for _____

a. there

b. car

~~c. shirt~~

d. here

e. score

f. tour

In some words, every letter makes a sound.

     man ⟶ /m/ /æ/ /n/

In other words, not every letter makes a separate sound.

     make ⟶ /m/ /eɪ/ /k/

E. Write the number of sounds in each word. Use a dictionary to check your answers.

1. __3__ take   2. _____ need   3. _____ loose

4. _____ knee   5. _____ now   6. _____ fun

7. _____ might   8. _____ too   9. _____ mouth

Rhyme

Some words have the same pattern of letters. The spelling is the same. The ending sounds are the same. The words rhyme.

     fake make bake take

Some words rhyme, but they have different letters. The spelling patterns are different.

     week speak

A. Say the words with a partner. Cross out the word that does not rhyme. Use a dictionary to check your answers.

1. night   kite   light   ~~sit~~   bite

2. feet   meat   street   cheat   cent

3. laid   mad   made   afraid   grade

4. eight   late   maid   gate   wait

5. enjoys   voice   toys   boys   noise

Word sounds, spellings, and meanings

Some words sound the same, but the spellings are different.

to   too   two   /tu/

The words have different meanings.

*I am going **to** the park. I am coming **too**. **Two** people walk to the park.*

A. Write each bold word under the correct picture.

I need a cup of **flour** for the cake.	I picked a beautiful **flower** from my garden.
The **sun** is really hot today.	My **son** is five years old.
We have to fly on a **plane** to Mexico.	My bag is very **plain**. There are no designs or colors on it.

1.

2.

3.

4.

5.

6.

Some words have the same spelling. They sound the same, but their meanings are different.

*I enjoy **running**.*

*Did you leave the car **running**?*

B. Match each sentence to the correct picture.

1. I received a **letter** from my friend.
2. I think a **letter** is missing from the sign.
3. My **goal** is to graduate college.
4. My favorite player scored a **goal**!
5. I got a **cold** and have been sick for a week.
6. It's very **cold** today. I am wearing a hat and gloves.

Some words have the same spelling but different sounds and meanings.

I will **close** *the door.* /clouz/

I live **close** *to my school.* /clous/

C. Match each sentence to the correct picture.

1. She had **tears** coming down her face.
   /tɪrz/

2. She **tears** the tickets into pieces.
   /tɛrz/

3. I have to **wind** the clock to make it work.
   /waɪnd/

4. The **wind** is strong today.
   /wɪnd/

5. I **lead** the students to gym class every day.
   /lid/

6. The statue of the man on the horse is made of **lead**.
   /lɛd/

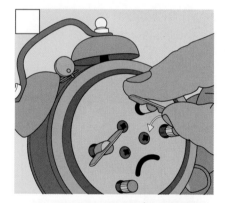

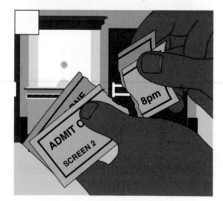

Stressed and unstressed syllables

Words are made of syllables. Each syllable has a vowel sound. Say each syllable in the words below:

read   lis•ten   un•der•stand
1   1   2   1   2   3

A. Write the number of syllables in each word.

1. these   their   after   learn   2. answer   try   connection   drink
    1

3. look   detail   partner   sentence   4. first   second   then   finally

In words with two syllables, one syllable is stressed. You say the vowel sound in the stressed syllable for a little longer than the other vowels.

B. Read each word. Stress the correct syllable.

1. i•DE-a   2. CON•so•nant   3. cor•RECT   4. be•LOW

In words with more than two syllables, one syllable has strong stress. Another syllable can also have stress, but it is not as strong. Its stress is weak.

1   2   3   4
con•ver•SA•tion

The third syllable has strong stress. The first syllable has weak stress.

C. The schwa /ə/ sound is not stressed. Read each word with the schwa. Stress the correct syllable. Say the vowel sound in that word longer.

1. a•BOUT   2. FA•ther   3. NUM•ber   4. o•PIN•ion

D. Draw a line to show the syllables in each word. Then underline the stressed syllable.

1. bet|ter   2. reason   3. people   4. happen   5. different

E. Match each word to a word with the same number of syllables and the same syllable with strong stress.

1. others   c   a. world

2. mystery _____   b. entertain

3. text _____   c. country

4. understand _____   d. history

5. exciting _____   e. instructions

Nouns

Some nouns name people, places, and things. We call them *concrete nouns* because you can see them.

teacher (person)   park (place)   cars (things)

A. Fill in the missing letters to spell each concrete noun. Use a dictionary for help.

1. bu_s_ _i_ _n_ _e_ss

2. co___p___te___

3. s___ud___n___

4. ne___sp___pe___

5. scie___ti___ ___

6. rest___ur___ ___t

Other nouns name ideas or feelings. We call them *abstract nouns* because you can't see them. The words below are abstract nouns.

sadness: *the feeling of being sad or upset*

success: *doing or getting what you wanted*

skill: *the ability to do something well*

B. Read each definition. Fill in the missing letters to spell each abstract noun. Use a dictionary if needed.

1. ed_u_c_a_tion: the ideas people learn at a school or college

2. hap___ine___s: the feeling of being good and pleased

3. re___ati___ns___ip: the way people or groups act or behave with each other

C. For each abstract noun in Activity B, list three concrete nouns related to it.

1. library, school, books _____

2. _____

3. _____

Many abstract nouns have common word endings. These word endings are called *suffixes*. You can identify which words are nouns by identifying their suffixes.

Suffix	Word	Meaning
-ance, -ence	perform**ance**	the act of performing
-ation, -tion, -ion	transport**ation**	the act of transporting
-ment	achieve**ment**	the result of achieving
-ness	ill**ness**	the quality of being ill
-ility, -ity	possib**ility**	the quality of being possible

D. Which words are nouns? Look for suffixes. Circle the noun or nouns in each row.

1. scratch ⟨responsibility⟩ demonstrate rise

2. solution take happy science

3. statement sad their weakness

4. awake appearance think always

5. importance question ask write

There are two kinds of nouns in English, count and noncount nouns. Count nouns are things you can count. You can tell how many there are. Noncount nouns are for things you can't count.

E. Circle the nouns in each sentence. Then write each noun in the correct column.

1. The air is cool near the mountains.   2. I need to buy some milk and also get two cans of soup.

3. The stars in the sky shine bright.   4. I have one brother and two sisters.

Count Nouns	Noncount Nouns
mountains	

Adjectives

Some words are adjectives. They describe nouns. Adjectives can be numbers, colors, and describing words to tell about size, feelings, or other characteristics.

three *girls*

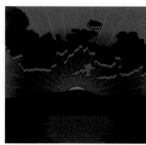
purple *sky*

large *truck*

hard *floor*

A. Look at each picture. Write a phrase to describe it with an adjective from the box.

| beautiful | interesting | new | old | ~~white~~ | young |

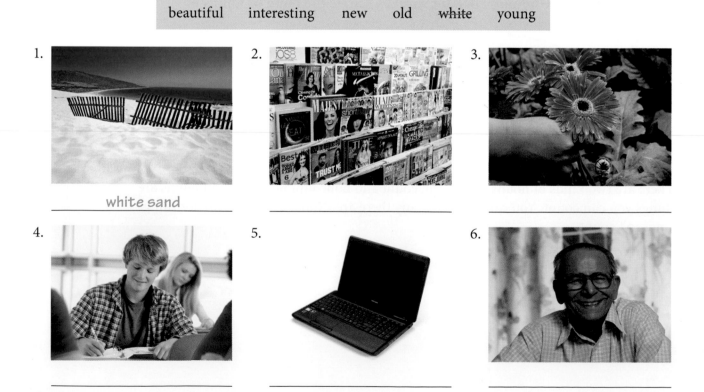

1. _____white sand_____

2. _____

3. _____

4. _____

5. _____

6. _____

B. Look at each picture. Write an adjective to tell about the noun. Use the Oxford 2000 list on page 133 to help you.

1. _____ boy   2. _____ building   3. _____ flowers

You can also identify adjectives from suffixes.

Suffix	Word	Meaning
-able,-ible	*valu**able***	having value
-al, -ial	*financ**ial***	relating to finance
-ful	*success**ful***	full of success
-ious, -ive, -ous	*danger**ous***	having danger

C. Which words are adjectives? Look for suffixes. Circle the adjective or adjectives in each row.

1. (famous)   person   give   (wonderful)

2. doctor   generous   probable   question

3. reasonable   mysterious   relation   connection

4. unable   obvious   statement   helpful

5. international   number   poisonous   possible

Verbs

Some words are verbs. Some verbs show action. They tell what nouns do. Other verbs tell what nouns are. We call these verbs *linking verbs* because they link a noun to another noun or adjective.

A. Fill in the missing letters to spell each action verb. Use a dictionary for help.

1. im_a_g_i_ne   2. st__d__   3. l__s__en

B. Circle each linking verb.

1. My dad (is) funny.

2. My mom was a scientist.

3. The books are on the table.

4. We were friends.

Verb tenses

The *tense* of a verb shows when something happened.

Add *-s* to verbs in the present tense when the subject is singular.

> *understand + -s = She understands.*

We also use present tense for things that always happen.

> *She goes to work at 8 every morning.*

We use past tense for things that happened before, in the past.

> *I called you yesterday.*

Some verbs are regular. Add *-ed* to regular verbs to form the past tense.

> *look + -ed = looked*

Other verbs are irregular. The past tense form is different from the present tense.

> *buy = bought*

A. Look at the present and past tense forms of the linking verb *be*. Notice how they are different.

	Present	Past
he/she/it	*is*	*was*
I	*am*	*was*
you	*are*	*were*
we	*are*	*were*
they	*are*	*were*

B. Circle the verb in each sentence.

Present Tense

1. I (am) happy today.

3. I go to the store every Saturday.

5. I make dinner at 7 p.m. each night.

7. He knows the answers.

9. I walk to the park in the morning.

11. She talks fast.

Past Tense

2. I (was) happy yesterday.

4. Yesterday, I went to the store.

6. I made dinner already.

8. He knew the answers.

10. I walked to the park on Tuesday.

12. She talked fast.

C. Write each verb from Activity B in the correct column.

Regular Verbs	Irregular Verbs	Forms of *be*
		am/was

D. Read the additional tenses and examples below.

Tense	Description	Example
present progressive	used to describe actions that are true right now but are not always true	*am/is/are* + verb + *-ing* I **am reading**.
present perfect	used to describe events that happened before now (not at a certain time)	*has/have* + past tense verb form I **have been** to Morocco.
past progressive	used to describe events that happened in the past but were stopped	*was/were* + verb + *-ing* I **was talking** on the phone when you called.
future	used to talk about events that will happen at a later time (in the future)	*will* + verb I **will study** later tonight.

E. Match each bold verb to the correct tense.

1. _f_ I **will work** late tonight.

2. _____ Paulo **told** me about the class.

3. _____ Katia **is** busy.

4. _____ We **are working** on our class project.

5. _____ I **have read** that book.

6. _____ We **were walking** to the store when it began to rain.

a. present

b. present progressive

c. present perfect

d. past

e. past progressive

f. future

▲▲▲ PHRASES, SENTENCES, AND PARAGRAPHS

Collocations

When you read, notice the words that appear together often. They are called *collocations*. These words go together. Learning collocations helps you write better sentences.

adjective noun
She has **strong opinions**. (not *powerful opinions*)

verb noun
I **do homework** every night. (not *make homework*)

A. Write each collocation below the correct picture.

> I **make mistakes** on my homework sometimes.
>
> I **have a question**.
>
> I **take notes** in class.
>
> I need to **make a phone call**.

1. _____

2. _____

3. _____

4. _____

Sentences

A sentence tells an idea. A sentence begins with a capital letter. If the sentence is a statement, it ends in a period. If it asks a question, it ends in a question mark. If it says something with feeling, it ends in an exclamation point.

A. Read the sentences with a partner. Then match each sentence to the correct picture.

1. I study every night.

2. Do you like to read on vacation?

3. What do you do for work?

4. This line is too long!

B. Write the number of the sentence from Activity A that matches each description.

_____ This sentence needs a *yes* or *no* answer.   _____ This sentence ends in a period.

_____ This sentence says something with feeling.   _____ This sentence needs more than a one-word answer.

Paragraphs

We use sentences to write paragraphs. The sentences in a paragraph talk about one thing. The paragraph has a main idea. The other sentences share details about the main idea.

A. Reorder the sentences to make a paragraph. Number the main idea *1* so it is the first sentence.

_____ First, many people learn it to find a job.

_____ People all over the world learn English.

_____ Think about why you are learning English.

_____ Second, some people learn it to do business.

_____ What do you want to do? How can it help you?

_____ Third, others learn it because their school teaches it.

B. Read the text. Then answer the questions.

Both writers and readers have purposes. People read for different reasons. Some people enjoy a good mystery. These stories are exciting. Something bad happened, but people don't know why. They read to find the answer. Other people like to read about history. They want to understand things from the past. Some enjoy reading about people. They like to think about people's lives. Other people read to see what is happening in the world. What do you like to read?

When you read, think about why the writer wrote the text. Some writers want to entertain people. They want people to enjoy the story and the language. Other writers write the facts. They want to report what happened. Some people share their writing to teach others. They tell how to do something. They give instructions. They share their opinions and thoughts. You can understand the writer's ideas when you know the writer's purpose. When you read, ask, "Why did the writer write this?"

People get meaning from the words in a text, but you can also learn from thinking about the text. It helps to understand why you read. Then you can choose texts for your purpose. Also try to understand why the writer wrote the text. The writer is a person talking to you. Enjoy the conversation.

1. The first paragraph uses the word *some*. Who does *some* refer to?

   a. texts   b. people   c. reading

2. Two words below have a similar meaning. Circle the word that is different.

   a. fact   b. thought   c. opinion

3. What is a good title for the text?

   a. "Read with Purpose"   b. "Why Do Writers Write?"   c. "Reading"

4. The text explains _____ .

   a. events from the past   b. people and their lives

   c. ideas to think about when you read

5. Which sentence best states the main idea of the text?

   a. People get meaning from the words in a text, but you can also learn from thinking about the text.

   b. When you read, think about why the writer wrote the text.

   c. People read for different reasons.

● Make Connections

Text to Self

When you make a connection to a text, you think about your life. You think about what you know.

A. Answer the questions.

1. What do you like to read? Why? _____

_____

2. What purposes do you read for? _____

_____

3. Why are you learning English? _____

_____

Text to Text

When you make connections between texts, you think about what they talk about. How are the texts the same? How are they different? What is each writer's purpose?

B. Look at the texts in Activity A on page 15 and Activity B on page 16. Complete the paragraph with the words from the box.

English	learning	purpose	reading	writing

Both texts talk about why someone does something. This is called

_____ . The first text talks about _____ English. It tells

the many reasons people study _____ . The second text talks about

_____ and _____ . Both texts explain something. They

also ask questions. They want the reader to think about his or her life.

Text to World

When you make a connection to the world, you think about the text and what you know about other texts, ideas, and writers in the world.

C. Answer the questions. Talk with a partner. Look at the Oxford 2000 keywords on page 133 and find more words to help you.

1. What texts do many people read? Why?

2. What purposes do writers write for?

3. Why do writers ask questions in their texts?

Look at the word bank for the Readiness Unit. Check (✓) the words you know. Circle the words you want to learn better.

OXFORD 2000 🔑

Adjectives	Nouns			Verbs
beautiful	beach	line	sadness	be
cold	business	mistake	scientist	close
happy	call	newspaper	skill	have
hard	car	note	son	imagine
interesting	cold	opinion	student	lead
large	computer	park	success	listen
new	education	phone	sun	make
old	fact	plane	teacher	read
plain	flour	purpose	tear	run
purple	flower	question	text	study
white	goal	relationship	thought	take
	happiness	restaurant	wind	tear
	letter	sentence		understand
				write

PRACTICE WITH THE OXFORD 2000 🔑

A. Use the words in the chart. Match adjectives with nouns.

1. _____beautiful beach_____   2. _____

3. _____   4. _____

5. _____

B. Use the words in the chart. Match verbs with nouns.

1. _____read the newspaper_____   2. _____

3. _____   4. _____

5. _____

C. Use the words in the chart. Match verbs with adjective noun partners.

1. _____write an interesting letter_____   2. _____

3. _____   4. _____

5. _____

UNIT 1 Learning and Behavior

CHAPTER 1 What Is Learning?

Reading 1: How Do We Learn?
Reading 2: Does Testing Help Us Learn?

BEFORE READING
- Oxford 2000 🔑 words to talk about learning
- *r*-controlled vowels

Make connections: Text to self

DURING READING
- Use a dictionary
- Identify cause and effect
- Present perfect to connect the past to the present; *or* to show different possibilities or choices

Make connections: Text to text

AFTER READING
Summarizing and retelling
Make connections: Text to world

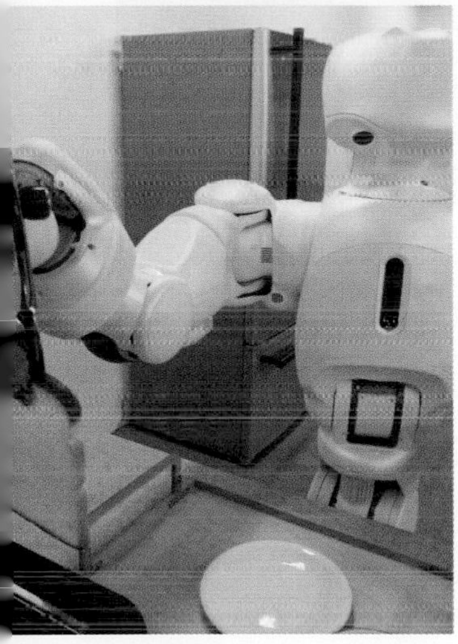

CHAPTER 2 How Is Technology Affecting Learning?

Reading 1: Can Robots Learn?
Reading 2: Do Video Games Teach?

BEFORE READING
- Oxford 2000 🔑 words to talk about technology and learning
- Schwa /ə/ in unstressed syllables

Make connections: Text to self

DURING READING
- Use vocabulary note cards
- Summarize ideas
- Adjective clauses with *where* and *if* to talk about possibility

Make connections: Text to text

AFTER READING
Summarizing and retelling
Make connections: Text to world

CHAPTER 3 Why Do We Do the Things We Do?

Reading 1: Why Do We Sleep?
Reading 2: Why Do We Laugh?

BEFORE READING
- Oxford 2000 🔑 words to talk about things we do
- *gh* as /f/ or as silent

Make connections: Text to self

DURING READING
- Collocations
- Skim for information and answers
- Quoted speech

Make connections: Text to text

AFTER READING
Summarizing and retelling
Make connections: Text to world

UNIT WRAP UP Extend Your Skills

What Is Learning?

- *r*-controlled vowels
- Use a dictionary
- Identify cause and effect

- Present perfect to connect the past to the present
- *or* to show different possibilities or choices

▲ **BEFORE READING** ► Oxford 2000 🔑 words to talk about learning

Learn Vocabulary

A. Match each picture to the correct sentence.

__1__ When you **concentrate**, you focus all your attention on something.

_____ The human **brain** has billions of nerve cells that send and receive information to all parts of the body.

_____ You answer questions on a **test** to show what you know or can do.

_____ A **memory** is something that happened in the past that you can think about now.

1.

2.
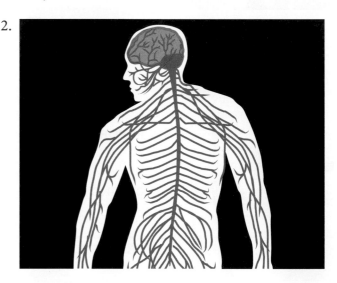

3.

4.
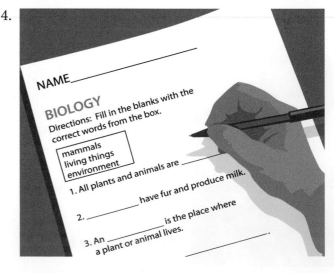

B. Match each sentence to the correct picture.

1. It is very **important** to wear a helmet when you ride a bicycle. It keeps you safe.

2. I can't **remember** where my car is.

3. Exercise has a **positive** effect on how people feel.

4. There is a **connection** between sleep and learning.

5. There are different **areas** of the school for small children and older kids.

6. **As a result** of my hard work, I did well on my paper!

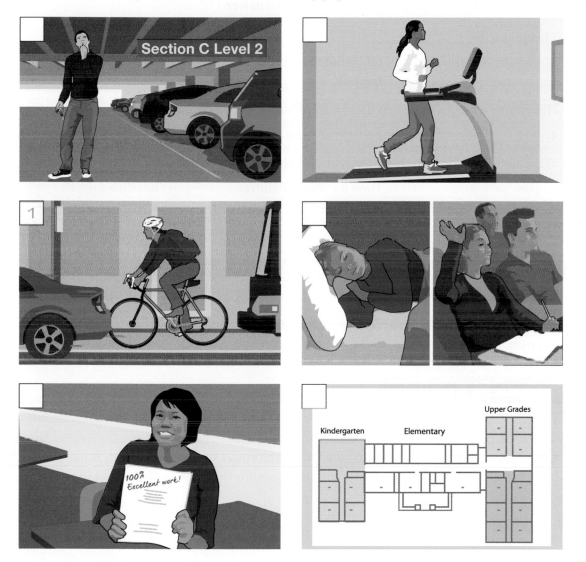

Oxford 2000

Use the Oxford 2000 list on page 133 to find more words to describe the pictures on these pages. Share your words with a partner.

C. Answer the questions with a partner.

1. What is a happy **memory** you have from your childhood?

2. Is it **important** to you to learn English?

3. Can you **concentrate** on studying while listening to music?

4. What do you **remember** about the last movie you watched?

5. Does taking **tests** make you nervous?

GO ONLINE for more practice

Preview the Text

D. Look at the picture on page 24. Answer the questions.

1. What do you think the person in the picture is doing? _____

_____

2. What is the person in the picture explaining? _____

_____

E. Look at the text on page 24. Circle the best answer.

1. This text will _____.

    a. explain something   b. tell about something in   c. describe a person
                                     the past

2. How many areas in the brain do you think are connected to learning?

    a. one   b. between 10 and 20   c. more than 20

3. Which question do you think the text will NOT answer?

    a. How do people   b. How do young children   c. What do adults like to
       remember new   learn?   learn?
       information?

4. Who do you think this text is written for?

    a. teachers and   b. doctors and people in the   c. young children
       students   medical field

5. What new word in the picture will be explained in the text?

    a. study   b. store   c. hippocampus

Sounds of English

Spelling Connection

A. When the letter *r* comes after a vowel, the vowel sound is different. It has an /r/ sound. The *r* controls the sound. Listen for the *r*-controlled vowel in each word below.

    burn   compare   dirt   effort   partner

B. Listen to the words. Circle the words that have an *r*-controlled vowel.

    area   important   remember   test

C. These words are in the text on page 24. Circle two words that have an *r*-controlled vowel.

    creating   different   ready   story

● Make Connections: Text to Self

A. Answer the questions. Use the bold words from pages 20–21 in your answers.

1. What do people do to learn something? _____

_____

2. Why can you remember some information but not everything? _____

_____

3. Write two important things people do to remember information. _____

_____

4. How long do you think most adults can concentrate? _____

_____

5. What things affect how long someone can concentrate? _____

_____

B. Think about how you learn. Complete the web.

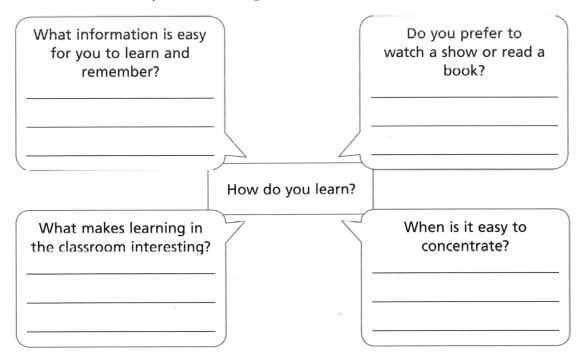

What information is easy
for you to learn and
remember?

_____

_____

_____

Do you prefer to
watch a show or read a
book?

_____

_____

_____

How do you learn?

What makes learning in
the classroom interesting?

_____

_____

_____

When is it easy to
concentrate?

_____

_____

_____

**C. Compare your answers from Activity B with a partner. Then discuss the
question below.**

Do you think most people learn in the same way?

🔊 Reading 1

A. Reading words in phrases or chunks can help you understand. Listen to the text. Mark the pauses you hear between phrases in long sentences in the first paragraph.

How Do We Learn?

Scientists have known for a long time that learning happens in different **areas** of the **brain**. Now, they think learning may involve as many as 50 areas! Learning is complicated. However, there is new research that can help us understand how we learn best. Think about learning in the classroom. If a teacher says, "The *hippocampus* in the brain helps in creating new **memories**," you may store, or keep, this new word and information. However, if you really want to **remember** this fact, it is best to make a **connection** to it. For instance, the teacher tells a story about someone whose hippocampus was damaged. **As a result**, the person can't create new memories. This will probably make you feel sad. Because you connect this fact to a story and an emotion, you involve different areas of your brain. The effect is you remember the new information better.

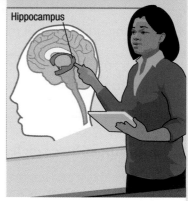
Hippocampus

There's another **important** part to learning: time. Time is important because you need time to **concentrate** in order to learn. Children can only concentrate for a short time. For most children, it is about one minute for each year of their age times three. For example, following this, a five-year-old can concentrate for about 15 minutes. However, other things affect how long you can concentrate. Return to the example of the classroom. If the teacher shares facts about the brain and then continues to share more and more facts, the result is the brain can't concentrate. This is because the information was repetitive: fact, fact, fact. However, if the teacher gives a fact, tells a story, and gives another fact, then different areas of the brain are involved. You don't lose concentration. You connect the fact to a story and an emotion. You remember it, and your brain takes a break from storing all the facts. Due to this, you can concentrate longer. Now, this doesn't mean teachers should tell story after story. The idea here is to provide different types of information to affect different areas of the brain. This is especially important for very young children. Their brains respond to different smells, materials, and colors five times more than adults. Show a bright color to children or give them toys or materials with different smells. The effect is the brain focuses. It's ready to learn.

Stop and Think

When you lose something, you don't have it anymore. What do you think *lose concentration* means?

B. Now read the text on your own. Focus on reading phrases or chunks of words to understand.

Check Your Understanding

C. Write _T_ (true) or _F_ (false). Rewrite false statements to be true.

1. __F__ There are 20 areas of the brain involved in learning.

There may be more than 50 areas of the brain involved in learning.

2. _____ The best way for a teacher to teach new information is to share many facts.

_____

3. _____ In general, a three-year-old child can concentrate for 15 minutes.

_____

4. _____ When you involve different areas of your brain, you learn better.

_____

5. _____ An example of how people store new information best is to hear a fact followed by a story that they connect to an emotion.

_____

Vocabulary Strategy

Use a Dictionary

Use a dictionary to help you understand new words from a text. This will help you better understand what you read. Before you use the dictionary, ask yourself two questions.

1. Is the word important to the text? Concentrate on the words that are most important.

2. Can I guess the meaning of the word from the text? Try to understand the word's meaning. Then use the dictionary to check your understanding.

Use a dictionary to find the pronunciation, the part of speech, the definitions, and example sentences of a new word. _Important!_ Find the definition that matches the use of the word from the text.

GO ONLINE
for more
practice

D. Look at the dictionary entry for _emotion_. Match each item to its description.

1. __e__ noun

2. _____ /ɪˈmoʊʃn/

3. _____ e•mo•tion

4. _____ a strong feeling, for example love or anger

5. _____ They expressed mixed emotions at the news.

> **e·mo·tion** 🔊 /ɪˈmoʊʃn/ _noun_ [count, noncount]
> a strong feeling, for example love or anger:
> _They expressed mixed emotions at the news._ ♦ _His voice was filled with emotion._

from _Oxford Basic American Dictionary_, 2011

a. example sentence   b. pronunciation   c. definition

d. syllables   ~~e. part of speech~~

Identify Cause and Effect

Cause-and-effect relationships are used in many kinds of text. Understanding them is important to the meaning of the text. A cause tells why something happened. The effect tells what happened.

cause ⟶ effect

Because *I studied,* *I did well on my test.*

Use signal words to help you identify the cause and effect. The signal word comes before the cause or effect.

Cause	Effect
as a result	leads to
because	the effect is
due to	the result is / results in
since	then

GO ONLINE
for more
practice

E. Circle the signal words and underline the effect in each sentence or set of sentences.

1. For instance, the teacher tells a story about someone whose hippocampus was damaged. As a result, the person can't create new memories.

2. Because you connect this fact to a story and an emotion, you involve different areas of your brain.

3. Time is important because you need time to concentrate in order to learn.

4. If the teacher shares facts about the brain and then continues to share more and more facts, the result is the brain can't concentrate.

◉ Reading 2

A. Listen to the text. Notice the pauses.

Does Testing Help Us Learn?

Everyone knows that studying is **important**. To do well, you have to study. In a popular book called *Outliers*, the author Malcolm Gladwell argues that 10,000 hours of practice can make you good at anything. This idea of "practice makes perfect" has been around for a long time, and there are many examples to support it. Most years,

students from Korea score in the top five among countries on an international **test**. How do they do so well? They study. After a long school day, they go to a *hagwon* for additional lessons and test practice. About 75 percent of Korean students go to school and *hagwons* until late at night. And their **results** on the international test show the positive effect. However, other research doesn't support what is called *cramming* for tests. When you cram for a test, you study a lot for it. Often you stay up late the night before the test, trying to memorize all the information. Many universities teach classes in a way that supports this type of study. Students are given a test in the middle of the course or a final test. These tests cover months of content. But how does a student **remember** all of that information? And will the student remember any of it after the test is over?

New research shows that taking tests often is good for students. It can result in them learning and better remembering information. For example, a student reads an essay about the **brain**. The student remembers the information at first, but then what happens to it? If the student takes a test soon after reading, then he or she has to recreate the information. This act of remembering and thinking about the information leads to better **memory** and learning. This is true even if the student

Many students in Korea go to hagwons *to study and practice taking tests.*

gets some of the questions on the test wrong. It's the act of trying to remember that is important. Scientists aren't exactly sure why this is. It could be that when you remember the information, the **connections** in the brain become stronger. The effect is that the next time you think about the facts you studied, you can remember them better. Now, if a teacher gives you a quiz, don't get upset. She is trying to help you better remember the new content!

Stop and Think

Do you usually remember information you were tested on? What is the effect on learning of taking a test?

B. **Read the text on your own. Pause between phrases to help you read with understanding.**

Grammar in the Readings

Notice the present perfect to connect the past to the present in the readings.

Use the present perfect to talk about an event from the past that affects the present.

*Scientists **have known** for a long time that learning involves different areas of the brain. Now, they think there may be as many as 50 areas involved.*

*This idea of "practice makes perfect" **has been** around for a long time.*

Notice *or* to show different possibilities or choices in the readings.

Use *or* to show different possibilities or choices.

*Show a bright color to children **or** give them toys **or** materials with different smells.*

*Students are given a test in the middle of the course **or** a final test.*

GO ONLINE
for grammar practice

Check Your Understanding

C. Circle the best answer.

1. What does *practice makes perfect* mean?

   a. If you practice, you will do very well.

   b. If you do well, you do not need to practice.

   c. It is not possible to be perfect.

2. Which statement is true?

   a. Taking a test helps even when the student answers incorrectly.

   b. Taking a test helps only when students d well on the test.

   c. Taking a test is not helpful for students.

3. Which statement does the text support?

   a. Give students one final test.

   b. Give students many tests.

   c. Do not give students tests.

4. What happens in the brain when you take test?

   a. You can't remember the information.

   b. You make the connections in your brain stronger.

   c. Your brain can't concentrate.

5. What does *cram* mean?

   a. to take tests often

   b. to not study

   c. to study a lot

Recycle

the Vocabulary Strategy

Vocabulary Strategy: Use a Dictionary

D. Look at the dictionary entries for *content*. Circle the correct answer.

1. What part of speech is the word *content* in the text on pages 26–27?

   a. adjective   b. noun

2. Which definition matches the use of the word *content* in the text on pages 26–27?

   a. 1   b. 2

3. Which pronunciation matches *content* from the text on pages 26–27?

   a. /ˈkɑntɛnt/   b. /kənˈtɛnt/

> **con·tent**[1] /kənˈtɛnt/ *adjective*
> happy or satisfied with what you have: *She is not content with the money she has – she wants more.*
> **con·tent**[2] /ˈkɑntɛnt/ *noun*
> **1** contents [*plural*] what is inside something: *I poured the contents of the bottle into a bowl.* ◆ *The contents page of a book tells you what is in it.*
> **2** [*singular*] the main ideas or facts in a book, an essay, a speech, etc.: *The content of the essay is good, but there are too many spelling mistakes.*

from *Oxford Basic American Dictionary*, 2011

Recycle

the Reading Strategy

Reading Strategy: Identify Cause and Effect

E. Circle the signal words and underline the cause in each sentence or set of sentences.

1. If the student takes a test soon after reading, then he or she has to recreate the information.

2. This act of remembering and thinking about the information leads to better memory and learning.

3. It could be that when you remember the information, the connections in the brain become stronger. The effect is that the next time you think about the facts you studied, you can remember them better.

● Make Connections: Text to Text

A. Think about the two texts. Circle the best answer.

1. Both texts use cause and effect. Why?

   a. to give reasons and explanations

   b. to give descriptions and characteristics

   c. to describe people and places

2. What question do both texts answer?

   a. How does it work?

   b. What did the person do?

   c. What is it like?

3. What topic are both texts connected to?

   a. history

   b. learning and education

   c. a person's life

4. Both texts include research. Why?

   a. to include details about opinions

   b. to tell an interesting story

   c. to support ideas with facts

B. Both texts give support and examples. Match the example to the idea it supports.

Ideas

1. _____ If you really want to remember a fact, it is best to make a connection to it.

2. _____ Children can only concentrate for a short time.

3. _____ To do well, you have to study.

4. _____ This act of remembering and thinking about the information leads to better memory and learning.

Support and Examples

a. A five-year-old can concentrate for about 15 minutes.

b. If the student takes a test soon after reading, then he or she has to recreate the information.

c. The teacher tells a story about someone whose hippocampus was damaged. As a result, the person can't create new memories. This will probably make you feel sad.

d. About 75 percent of Korean students go to school and *hagwons* until late at night. And their results on the international test show the positive effect.

AFTER READING

Summarizing and Retelling

A. Complete the sentences with the words from the box. Some of the words have to be changed to fit the sentences. For example, *area* has to be changed to *areas*. Then read the paragraphs to a partner to retell the ideas.

Adjectives	Nouns	Verbs
important positive	area brain connection memory result test	concentrate remember

1. In "How Do We Learn?" the writer discusses how we learn. She says it is best to

    make _____. Then you involve different _____ of

    your brain. As a(n) _____, you can better remember the information.

    Time is also _____ to learning. The length of time we can

    _____ is connected to our age.

2. In "Does Testing Help Us Learn?" the writer discusses what happens when students

    take _____ often. Research shows they learn better and

    _____ the information. The effect is _____. This is

    because when you take a test, you recall the information from your

    _____ and the connections in your _____ become

    stronger.

Word Partners

concentrate hard

concentrate on

can't concentrate

hard to concentrate

GO ONLINE
to practice
word partners

B. In both texts, the writer discusses research on the brain. Complete the chart to summarize the research.

Text | Research

"How Do We Learn?" →

"Does Testing Help Us Learn?" →

C. Look at the collocations with the word *research*. Use the collocations to summarize the research from each text. Discuss your ideas with a partner.

| important research | interesting research | new research | scientific research |

Example: *New research on the brain shows that…*

● Make Connections: Text to World

A. Think about the two texts. Answer the questions.

1. Who is the audience for these texts? For example, who do you think the texts would have a positive effect on? _____

_____

2. List other topics that include research. _____

_____

3. What other research areas often discuss causes and effects? _____

_____

4. When should you use a dictionary? _____

_____

B. What effect do you think each text has on teachers? For example, how might the texts affect their teaching? Complete the chart.

Text   Effect on Teachers

"How Do We Learn?" ⟶ _____
                        _____

"Does Testing Help Us Learn?" ⟶ _____
                                  _____

C. Talk with a partner. What do you want to learn about the brain? List three questions you want scientists to research. Look at the Oxford 2000 keywords on page 133 and find five words to help you.

1. _____

_____

2. _____

_____

3. _____

_____

Chant

GO ONLINE for the Chapter 1 Vocabulary & Grammar Chant

How Is Technology Affecting Learning?

- Schwa /ə/ in unstressed syllables
- Use vocabulary note cards
- Summarize ideas
- Adjective clauses with *where* and *if* to talk about possibility

▲ **BEFORE READING** ▶ Oxford 2000 ✎ words to talk about technology and learning

Learn Vocabulary

A. Read the definitions and look at the picture. Complete the paragraph with the bold words from the box.

experiment: a scientific test to find out what will happen	**similar:** when two things are alike
predicts: to say what you think will happen	**objects:** things you can see and touch
model: a person or thing that is an example	**task:** something you need to do

In this _____ , the boy is testing to see which _____ sink quickly.

He _____ that the heaviest objects will sink the fastest. He uses his science book as a

_____ for how to do the experiment. It shows what he needs to do for each step, or

_____ . Will _____ objects sink at the same speed?

B. Match each sentence to the correct picture.

1. There are many **benefits to** technology. One is that you can communicate with people all over the world.

2. He **controls** the player's actions in the video game.

3. I have to **identify** the correct answer, but I'm not sure what it is.

4. My **reaction** to the game ending was bad. I was upset.

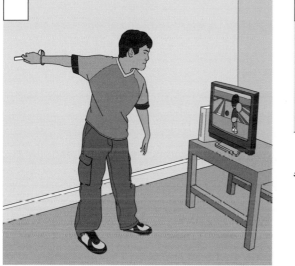

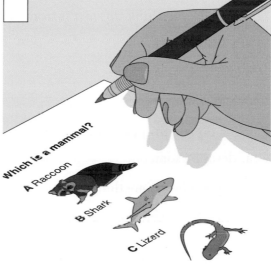

Oxford 2000 🔑

Use the Oxford 2000 list on page 133 to find more words to describe the pictures on these pages. Share your words with a partner.

C. Answer the questions with a partner.

1. What is your **reaction to** losing a game?

2. How do you **control** your reactions when you are upset? **Identify** two ways you can better control them.

3. What **benefits** are there **to** video games?

4. What things do people often **predict**?

5. Why do people do **experiments**?

GO ONLINE for more practice

Preview the Text

D. Look at the pictures and text on page 36. Circle the correct answer.

1. What is a robot?

    a. a machine that can work like a person

    b. a person that works with technology

    c. a piece of furniture, like a chair

2. Where do you think this text is from?

    a. a history book

    b. a science magazine

    c. a business report

3. What do you think the text will do?

    a. describe someone

    b. explain how something works

    c. tell why something happens

E. Read the title. Write a sentence you think might be in the text. Use two of the bold words from pages 32–33 in your sentence.

_____

_____

Sounds of English

Spelling Connection

A. In words with more than one syllable, some syllables are stressed. You say the vowel sound longer in these syllables. Other syllables are unstressed. Often, the unstressed syllable has a schwa /ə/ sound. It is a short sound. Listen for the schwa in the words below.

about   adult   children   connection

B. Listen to the words. Circle the words that have an unstressed syllable with the schwa sound. Underline the letter that makes the schwa sound.

benefit   control   experiment   identify   task

● Make Connections: Text to Self

A. Answer the questions.

1. What tasks do robots do? _____

_____

2. Have you seen, used, or worked with a robot? Describe what happened. _____

_____

3. Do you think in the future you will use a robot at home or work? Why or why not?

_____

_____

4. Do you think the way robots learn is similar to humans? Why or why not? _____

_____

B. Imagine you can have a robot to help you. What tasks do you want the robot to do? Complete the web.

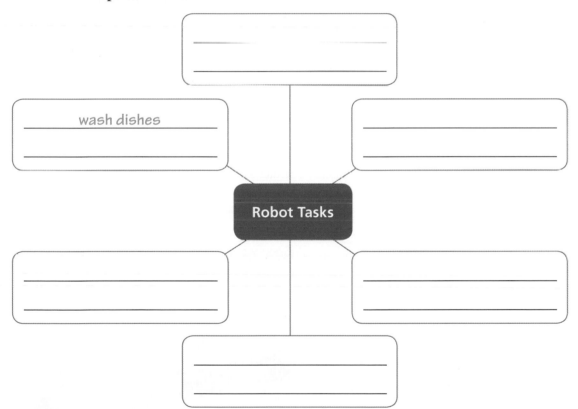

C. Compare your answers from Activity B with a partner. Then discuss the question below.

Why don't we have robots to do these tasks?

🔊 Reading 1

A. Listen to the text. Listen for the stressed syllables in words with more than one syllable.

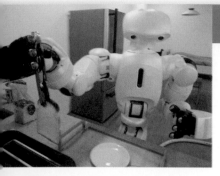

This robot can perform actions like opening doors, throwing away garbage, and picking up cups.

Can Robots Learn?

In 1964, science fiction writer Isaac Asimov **predicted**: (1) Technology will do the jobs of workers; (2) We will be able to see the people we talk to on the phone; (3) There will be robots in 2014, but they won't be that good. These were some of his predictions that have come true. While many people have heard about robots that work, not everyone has actually seen one. Why aren't robots common? Why do we have technology that allows us to see people we talk to, but not robots to help with **tasks** at home and work? Well, there are robots to do simple jobs. One popular robot vacuums a room on its own. Other robots complete tasks to help build cars and other technology. However, most robots now can only do one thing. And even with this one task, they don't always work correctly. The question is "Can we teach robots to do more than one thing?" Can robots learn?

New **experiments** show that robots can learn. In one experiment, a robot learned to **identify** if an **object** was a container. The robot dropped a block onto an object. If the object was a container, the block would fall inside it. If the object was not a container, the block would fall to the side. Then the robot pushed the object. The robot used its camera to see if the block moved with the object. If it did, the robot

identified it as a container because the two things moved together. It had learned! And it could use this information to predict if an object could hold something. The robot showed that it could test objects, learn about them, and identify other objects that had the same characteristics. This is **similar** to how humans learn.

What does this mean for the future? It shows that robots are learning like us and even learning from us. One robot that scientists are developing uses people as a **model**. It learns from watching. For example, it studies how a person moves and predicts where the person will move next. The robot then uses this information to move around the person. This robot also watches how people hold and use objects. Then it performs tasks, like opening doors and throwing away garbage. For years, people have predicted our use of robots. Soon we may find them in our homes and workplaces, quiet students studying our every move.

This robot vacuums rooms.

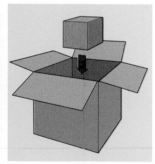

A container is different from a block. It can hold something.

Stop and Think

Can you think of examples of containers?

B. Now take turns reading the paragraphs with a partner. Concentrate on stressing the correct syllables in words with more than one syllable.

Check Your Understanding

C. Circle the best answer.

1. The main idea is
   _____ .

   (a.) robots can learn

   b. robots will soon take your job

   c. Isaac Asimov made correct predictions

2. The writer says robots now can do simple jobs. What is an example?

   a. a robot that predicts where a person will move

   b. a robot that learns like a human

   c. a robot that vacuums a room

3. The way that _____ is similar.

   a. robots and humans move

   b. robots and humans learn

   c. robots and objects move

4. The text does not support the statement that
   _____ .

   a. robots can learn from watching humans

   b. robots can learn from watching other robots

   c. robots can learn from doing an experiment

Vocabulary Strategy

Use Vocabulary Note Cards

Create vocabulary note cards for the words you are learning. Use the cards to test your learning. This will help you remember new words.

part of speech   examples   example sentence   new word

(n.) a thing that you can put other things in

Ex.: boxes, bottles, cups

I need a container for the food I didn't eat.

Word family: contain *(v.)*

Word partners: container of, empty/full container

container

collocations   word from the same family

Write the word on the front of the card and the part of speech, its meaning, a small picture if possible, and an example sentence on the back. You may also want to write examples, words in the same word family, collocations, and the word in your first language.

GO ONLINE for more practice

D. Use a dictionary and your own ideas to complete the information for the back of the vocabulary note card.

prediction _____ what someone thinks will happen

Ex.: _____

My prediction is we will have a quiz in English class tomorrow.

Word family: _____

Word partners: _____

Summarize Ideas

When you summarize ideas, you use your own words to retell main ideas from the text. Summarize ideas to check your understanding and answer questions. Summarizing ideas is important both in speaking and in writing. Use these strategies to help you.

1. Reread the part of the text you want to better understand.

2. Ask yourself, "What is important?"

3. Think about what you might say to someone who hasn't read the text. Write a short sentence to explain.

GO ONLINE
for more
practice

E. Look at the first paragraph on page 36. Read the summary below. Then answer the questions with a partner.

Summary: We have robots, but they aren't that helpful. The writer of this text wants to know why we don't have robots that can better help us.

1. Does the summary tell the important ideas from the paragraph? _____

2. Are the sentences different from the text? _____

3. Is the summary shorter than the text? _____

4. Do you think information is missing from the summary? _____

If yes, what information is missing? _____

F. Summarize the parts of the text on page 36.

1. Read paragraph 2 and summarize the main idea. _____

_____

2. Read paragraph 3 and summarize the main idea. _____

_____

◉ Reading 2

A. Preview the text. Then read it on your own.

Do Video Games Teach?

Are video games bad? Some people say there is too much bad behavior in games, especially action video games. They say that children should not play these kinds of games and that young people should concentrate on communication and other important skills. However, more than half a billion people in the world play video games for more than an hour each day! What is the effect on people? Are there any **benefits to** playing video games?

One research study showed that playing action video games causes changes in some areas of the brain. One area

controls working memory, where we store information we learn. We use working memory to make decisions. The other area controls hand-eye coordination. This is our physical **reaction to** things we see. Another study also showed the benefits. In this **experiment**, people completed a **task** of **identifying** patterns. People who played action video games did better than those who did not play the games. Why is this? The study said that people are always **predicting** what will happen. This is true for any task throughout the day. For example, if you are in a conversation or listening to your teacher, you often predict what the person will say. You also do this when driving. You predict how other drivers will move. The idea is that people are always creating **models** using their past experiences. This

helps people react quickly because they have an idea of what will happen. For example, after hearing a teacher talk, you may predict that she will now assign homework. Because of this, you get out your notebook and prepare to write the homework assignment down.

Action video game players get lots of practice predicting. They play a game and build models for what happens in different situations. The result is that they become good at quickly predicting what will happen. Due to this, they do better on video games and at other learning tasks. Some people point out the negative effects of video games, but the numbers show the world will continue to play them. And if it's an action game, it may help us learn.

Stop and Think

The writer defines *hand-eye coordination*. What tasks require hand-eye coordination?

Grammar in the Readings

Notice adjective clauses with *where* and *if* to talk about possibility in the readings.

Use adjective clauses with *where* to give more information about a place or area.

> *One area controls working memory,* **where we store information we learn**.

Use *if* to talk about possibility.

> *The robot used its camera to see* **if the block moved with the object. If it did**, *the robot identified it as a container because the two things moved together.*

> *For example,* **if you are in a conversation or listening to your teacher**, *you often predict what the person will say.*

GO ONLINE
for grammar practice

Check Your Understanding

B. Circle the correct answer.

1. Why don't some people like video games?

   a. They think games show bad behavior.

   b. They think children learn communication skills.

   c. They think many people play them.

2. Which statement does the text NOT support?

   a. When you play action games, you predict what will happen. This helps in other tasks.

   b. When you play action games, you use hand-eye coordination.

   c. When you play action games, you have a lot of fun.

3. Which is not an example of an action video game?

   a. a car racing video game

   b. a spelling video game

   c. a basketball video game

4. Why is creating a model of something in your head important?

   a. You use that information to make a prediction and react quickly.

   b. You play action video games more often.

   c. You can remember information better.

Vocabulary Strategy: Use Vocabulary Note Cards

Recycle

the Vocabulary Strategy

C. Use a dictionary and your own ideas to complete the information for the back of the vocabulary note card.

happen (*v.*) _____

Ex.: _____

Example sentence: _____

Word family: _____

Word partners: happen to, happen to do something

Reading Strategy: Summarize Ideas

Recycle

the Reading Strategy

D. Write the number of the paragraph from pages 38–39 that matches the summary.

1. _____ When you play action video games, you make predictions and this helps people learn. The effect of these types of games is positive.

2. _____ Research studies show that action video games have positive effects on some areas of the brain. In addition, a study supports the idea that they help us make predictions quickly.

3. _____ Some people think video games do not have positive effects. However, many people play them. The main question the writer asks is "Are there benefits to video games?"

⬤ Make Connections: Text to Text

A. Both texts answer a question and provide supporting details. Complete the chart with details that support the summary statements.

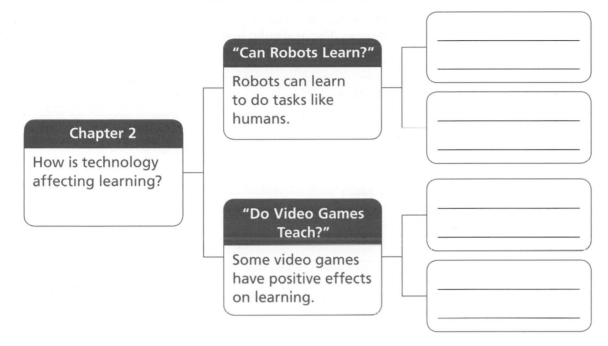

Chapter 2

How is technology affecting learning?

"Can Robots Learn?"

Robots can learn to do tasks like humans.

"Do Video Games Teach?"

Some video games have positive effects on learning.

B. Look at the supporting details you wrote in Activity A. Do they do a good job of supporting the summary statement? Is there enough information to support each main idea? Discuss with a partner.

C. Both texts talk about the situation now. Then at the end they discuss the future. Complete the chart.

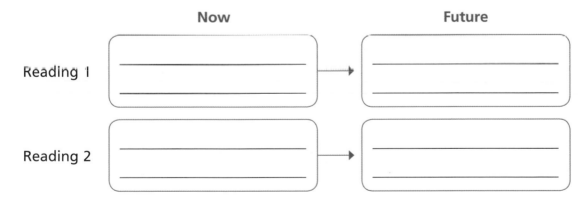

Now   Future

Reading 1

Reading 2

Summarizing and Retelling

A. Complete the questions with the words from the box. Some of the words have to be changed to fit the sentences. For example, *benefit* has to be changed to *benefits*.

Adjectives	Nouns	Verbs
similar	benefit experiment model object reaction task	control identify predict

1. What _____ did a robot use to learn if a(n) _____ was a container?

2. How did the robot _____ if the object was a container?

3. What _____ can robots do that are _____ to humans?

4. What _____ are there to playing video games?

5. Is the area of the brain that _____ working memory affected by playing action video games?

6. How does creating a(n) _____ help people learn?

7. How do video games affect your _____ to things you see?

8. Throughout the day, do you _____ what will happen next? How does this prediction help you learn?

B. Ask and answer the questions from Activity A with a partner. Reread the texts on pages 36 and 38–39 if you need help.

Word Partners

real benefits

great benefits

enjoy benefits

have benefits

social benefits

financial benefits

_____

GO ONLINE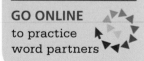
to practice
word partners

● Make Connections: Text to World

A. The texts support some of the statements below. What do you think? Check the statements you agree with.

"Can Robots Learn?"

1. _____ Robots can learn to do everything humans can do.

2. _____ Robots can learn from watching people.

3. _____ Robots can do things better than humans.

4. _____ Robots will soon do many jobs that humans do.

5. _____ Robots will be smarter than humans.

"Do Video Games Teach?"

6. _____ People who play action video games are better at learning.

7. _____ Playing any video game is good for you.

8. _____ Playing action video games will make you smarter.

9. _____ In the future, people will use video games to learn instead of books.

10. _____ Research will find that playing video games has negative effects.

B. Discuss your answers from Activity A with a partner. Think of examples to support your ideas. Look at the Oxford 2000 keywords on page 133 and find five words to help you.

C. Think of a question to ask the writer of each text. What do you want to know more about? What information do you wish was in the text?

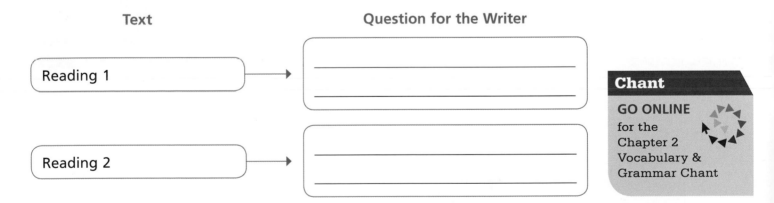

Text   Question for the Writer

Reading 1 ⟶ _____

Reading 2 ⟶ _____

Chant

GO ONLINE for the Chapter 2 Vocabulary & Grammar Chant

CHAPTER 3

Why Do We Do the Things We Do?

- *gh* as /f/ or as silent
- Collocations
- Skim for information and answers
- Quoted speech

▲ BEFORE READING ► Oxford 2000 🔑 words to talk about things we do

Learn Vocabulary

A. Match each picture to the correct definition.

_____ **Waste** is material or food that people no longer need or use.

_____ When you **repair** something, you make something that is broken or damaged good again.

_____ A **muscle** is a part in your body that is connected to the bone and helps you move.

___1___ A **system** is a group of things or parts that work together.

1.
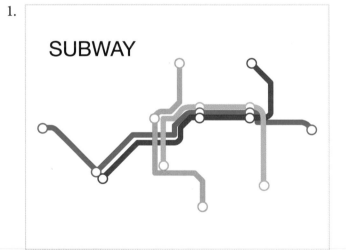

2.
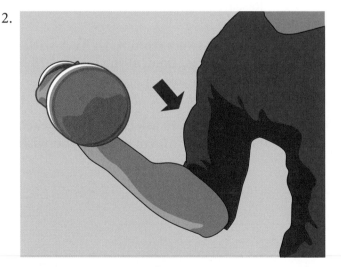

3.

4.

B. Match each description to the correct picture.

1. First, you go to bed. You want to get **enough sleep** for the next day so you feel good.

2. Once you are sleeping, you begin to **dream**. You see things from your day and other things that you may not understand.

3. In the morning, your alarm goes off. You turn it off. You feel **awake** and ready for the day.

C. Look at the picture. Complete the paragraph with the phrases from the box.

funny faces	~~sense of humor~~	tell a joke

My dad has a great _____sense of humor_____. He tells jokes that make everyone around him laugh. But what really makes people laugh are his

_____ . You have to see him _____ to

understand how funny he is.

GO ONLINE
for more
practice

Preview the Text

D. Look at the picture and text on page 48. Answer the questions.

1. The topic of the text is sleep. List three ideas you think the text will discuss. _____

_____

2. Why do you think the writer included a picture of an athlete in a text about sleep?

_____

_____

3. The title of the text is a *why* question. What words do you think the writer will use to

   answer this question? _____

_____

E. Look at the text on page 48. Answer the questions.

1. The second paragraph uses the phrase *get rid of waste*. This means "to take waste away." Cross out the phrase below that does NOT have a similar meaning.

   aware of   clearing out   throw away

2. The body has different systems. With a partner, discuss why the items below are systems.

   muscles

   breathing

   the brain

3. Underline a word that is another word for *brain*:

   In addition, dreams let the mind wander. Because of this, dreams may allow us to look for connections between things.

Sounds of English

Spelling Connection

🔊 A. Listen to the word *laugh*. What sound does the *gh* make? The *gh* can make the /f/ sound. But many times *gh* is silent. There is no sound. Listen to the words below and write them in the correct column in the chart.

| cough | enough | might | night | right |
| rough | sight | though | thought | weigh |

gh Makes the /f/ Sound	*gh* Is Silent (No Sound)

⬤ **Make Connections:** Text to Self

A. Answer the questions.

1. How many hours of sleep do you think people need each night? _____

2. List two reasons why we sleep. _____

_____

3. What parts of the body does sleep affect? _____

_____

B. Complete the web. Look at the Oxford 2000 keywords on page 133 and find words to help you.

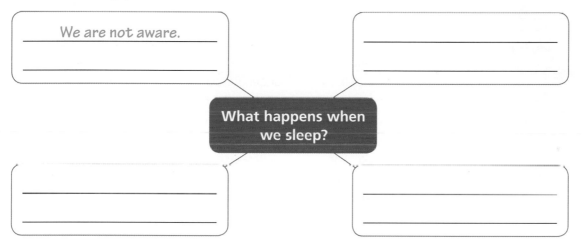

We are not aware.

What happens when we sleep?

C. Think about sleep. Complete the chart.

Sleep   Effect

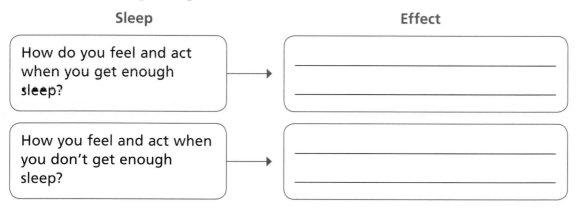

How do you feel and act when you get enough **sleep**?

How you feel and act when you don't get enough sleep?

◉ Reading 1

A. When we read, we say questions in a different way than statements. At the end of a question, your voice rises. At the end of a statement, your voice falls. This is called *intonation*. Listen to the text. Underline the questions.

Why Do We Sleep?

Olympic athlete Usain Bolt considers sleep an important part of his training. It gives him the energy he needs to win.

Stop and Think

What mistakes do we make without enough sleep?

What do people around the world do for about one-third of each day? **Sleep**. We spend a total of about 25 years of our life sleeping. It's as important as breathing. People who don't get sleep have many problems. Sleep affects us in ways we can feel, such as thinking and reacting more slowly, and in ways we aren't aware of. For instance, there are connections between not getting **enough** sleep and disease and illness. Do you know what happens when we sleep?

All the **systems** in the body use energy to work. **Muscles** work this way, as do other systems in the body. This is also true for the brain. Sleep allows the brain and the systems it controls to **repair** themselves. Then they have energy to work well the next day. It's also a time for the body to get rid of **waste** or other things that aren't good for it. **Dreams** may also be a way of clearing out what we don't need. In an interview, sleep researcher David Randall said, "Sleep is the time when our brain is allowed to kind of separate what's important from what it can kind of throw away." He explains that when we dream, we think about things we learned from the day before. We concentrate on what is important and let the other things go. We also dream about what is planned for the next day. We practice both what we learned and what we will do. In addition, dreams let the mind wander. Because of this, dreams may allow us to look for connections between things. The result is we are better thinkers after we sleep.

Research says that for every two hours you are **awake**, you need one hour of sleep. Yet many people are not getting enough sleep. In 2010, 30 percent of workers in the United States were getting less than six hours of sleep a night. Our understanding of sleep is based on what happens without it. People without enough sleep are less happy and get sick more often. It's hard to learn new things without enough sleep. Athletes without enough sleep don't do as well. They react more slowly. They also make more mistakes. When you lack sleep, your brain can't think quickly. Twenty percent of car accidents are caused by sleepy drivers. In one study, a person tried to stay awake for as long as possible. After two days, he could not do simple math problems. After eleven days, he didn't know who he was. Sleep affects both our mind and our body. Science shows we need it.

B. Read the text aloud. Use the right intonation on questions and statements.

Check Your Understanding

C. Complete the chart with the examples or facts for each supporting idea.

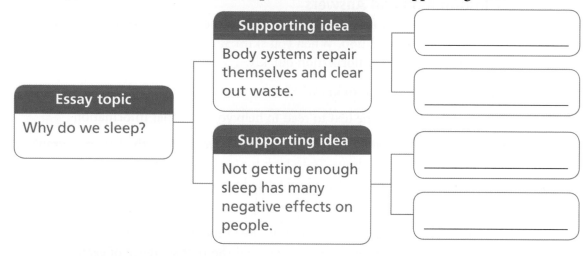

Essay topic

Why do we sleep?

Supporting idea

Body systems repair themselves and clear out waste.

_____

_____

Supporting idea

Not getting enough sleep has many negative effects on people.

_____

_____

Vocabulary Strategy

Collocations

Collocations are words that go together. Learning collocations will help you increase your vocabulary. There are collocations that are often used to talk about sleep.

For example, we don't take or make sleep. We **get sleep**.

Note that *sleep* is used as both a verb and a noun in collocations.

GO ONLINE for more practice

D. Read the text on page 48 again. Complete each collocation.

1. Athletes without _____*enough*_____ **sleep** don't do as well.

2. When you _____ **sleep**, your brain can't think quickly.

3. People who **don't** _____ **sleep** have many problems.

4. Research says that for every two hours you are awake, you _____ one hour of **sleep**.

5. In one study, a person tried to _____ **awake** for as long as possible.

E. Complete the sentences with the collocations from the box.

| lose sleep | good night's sleep | sleep in | can't sleep | ~~try to sleep~~ |

1. You have to _____*try to sleep*_____. It's late, and you need your rest.

2. Please don't wake me up tomorrow. I really want to _____.

3. Did you get a _____? You went to bed early, so I hope you feel rested.

4. You should go to bed. Don't _____ worrying about your test.

5. I drank too much coffee before bed, and now I _____.

Skim for Information and Answers

Use skimming to locate and find information in a nonfiction text. Nonfiction texts contain facts and true information. When you skim, it is OK not to read all the text. Skimming allows you to find information quickly.

1. First, identify what you want to know.

2. Then identify the parts of the text to read to help you find that information.

Use skimming to see if a text has the information you want. Read the first paragraph of the text. Find out what it is about. Then look for specific information you want to find in the other paragraphs. Don't read sentence by sentence. Instead look for key words to help you find the information you need.

Use skimming to find the answer to a question. Read the question. Identify key words that will help you find the answer. Then read the first sentence of each paragraph. Identify which paragraph you think will have the information. Look for the key words in the paragraph.

GO ONLINE
for more
practice

F. Underline key words in each question. Then skim the text on page 48 to find the answer and write it below.

1. How many <u>years</u> does a person spend <u>sleeping</u>?

_____

2. How many hours of sleep do we need for every two hours we are awake?

_____

3. What percentage of workers get less than six hours of sleep a night?

_____

4. What percentage of car accidents are caused by sleepy drivers?

_____

◉ Reading 2

A. Preview the text. Then read it to yourself.

Stop and Think

When do people laugh? What do they laugh at?

Why Do We Laugh?

When was the last time you laughed hard, really hard? Can you remember a time when you couldn't stop laughing? Babies first laugh when they are three and a half or four months old. The age people laugh the most is five or six. Maybe you remember a time from this age. What was so **funny**? While people often tell a **joke** to be funny, research shows people most often laugh at things that aren't so funny. For example, people laugh at simple statements that people use to begin a conversation—for example, "Here comes Hasid." Questions like "How did you do on your test?" can also cause laughter. This shows people laugh to be social. They want to make a connection with other people. In addition, this is why babies laugh. It's not that they are laughing at a funny face, but they too want to connect. Laughter is one of the first steps we take to be social. As an example, consider this joke: *What did the 0 say to the 8? Can I borrow your belt?* Did you laugh out loud? Probably not. We may read something or think something and laugh to ourselves. But laughter, the laugh out loud kind, is usually only done when other people are around. We laugh to be heard. We laugh to feel happiness and share it with others.

Laughter is not just a way to be social. It can connect or divide social groups. Someone laughs after a pause or after a sentence in a conversation. It's not a word but a way to respond, or say something back, and it communicates something. What does laughter say? "You're funny." "We share the same sense of **humor**." "I like you." "I'm listening to you." "I want to hear more." "I'm interested in you." There is a reason why one of the most used text messages that people send is an abbreviation for "laugh out loud": LOL. Of course, when we send this text message, we are not actually laughing out loud. We are communicating that we think the person is funny. However, laughing at someone is different. Laughter can be not nice. People use it to let someone know they don't belong. Laughter can make people feel part of a group or *not* part of the group.

When we hear someone laugh, we laugh too. Laughter is a response that we don't have to think about. It is passed from person to person. This is why TV shows use laugh tracks. The show includes a recording of an audience laughing. When TV viewers at home hear this, it makes them laugh too. And the laughter has an effect on our body. When we laugh, our face **muscles** move and our breathing changes. Muscles all over our body in our arms, core, and legs are affected. Laughter releases chemicals in the brain. They make us relax. We laugh and we feel good. We laugh and we feel a connection with others.

Laughter is a response we don't control. When we hear someone else laugh, we laugh too.

Grammar in the Readings

Notice quoted speech in the readings.

Writers use quoted speech to write the exact words people said. Recognizing quoted speech will help you understand who is communicating in a reading. Look at the punctuation on the quoted speech below.

In an interview, sleep researcher David Randall said, "Sleep is the time when our brain is allowed to kind of separate what's important from what it can kind of throw away."

What does laughter say? "You're funny." "We share the same sense of humor." "I like you." "I'm listening to you." "I want to hear more." "I'm interested in you."

GO ONLINE
for grammar
practice

Check Your Understanding

B. Write *T* (true) or *F* (false). Rewrite false statements to be true.

1. __F__ The reason people laugh is because jokes are really funny.
   We laugh to connect with others.

2. _____ Most people laugh when they are alone.

_____

3. _____ People laugh the most at age five or six.

_____

4. _____ Babies laugh because people are funny.

_____

Vocabulary Strategy: Collocations

Recycle

the Vocabulary
Strategy

C. Read the text on pages 50–51 again. Complete each collocation.

1. When was the last time you **laughed** _____hard_____, really hard?

2. Can you remember a time when you couldn't _____ **laughing**?

3. But laughter, the **laugh** _____ _____ kind, is usually only done when people are around.

4. However, **laughing** _____ **someone** is different.

Reading Strategy: Skim for Information and Answers

Recycle

the Reading
Strategy

D. Underline the key words in each question. Then skim the text on pages 50–51 to find the answer and write it below.

1. What is a statement people laugh at?

_____

2. What does *LOL* mean?

_____

3. What does laughter communicate?

_____

4. How does laughing affect the body?

_____

5. What is a laugh track?

_____

● Make Connections: Text to Text

A. Think about the two texts. Complete the chart.

Questions	Sleep	Laughter
What is the effect on the muscles?		
What is the effect on other systems in the body?		
What is the effect on the brain?		
How does it make you feel?		

B. The texts use similar writing techniques. Answer the questions.

1. The first sentence of the first paragraph in both texts is a question. Read the questions. Why does each writer begin with a question?

_____

2. The first paragraph in both texts introduces the topic. Write a sentence from the first paragraph in each text that you think best states the main idea of the text.

Reading 1: _____

Reading 2: _____

3. The second paragraph gives details to answer the question in the title. Write the sentence that you think best states the main idea for the second paragraph.

Reading 1: _____

Reading 2: _____

4. Both writers use two sentences to state the most important points of the text. Write the two most important sentences from each text.

Reading 1: _____

_____

Reading 2: _____

_____

Summarizing and Retelling

A. Complete the sentences with the words from the box. Some of the words have to be changed to fit the sentences. For example, *system* has to be changed to *systems*. Then read the paragraphs to a partner to summarize.

Adjectives	Nouns	Verbs
awake	humor	dream
enough	joke	repair
funny	muscle	
	sleep	
	system	
	waste	

1.　　We have to get _____ _____ because the body

needs time to _____ muscles. It also clears out _____

while we sleep. For every two hours we are _____ , we need one hour

of sleep. Time to dream is also important. When we _____ , we

practice what we learned that day.

2.　　When someone tells a(n) _____ or makes a(n)

_____ face, people laugh. However, the main reason we laugh is to be

social. We laugh so we can feel a connection to others. We show we have the same

sense of _____ .

3.　　In each text, the writer describes why we do the things we do. The writers describe

the effect of sleep and laughter on _____ in our body and other body

_____ . Both sleeping and laughing help us feel good.

B. Think about the two texts. Answer the questions.

1. Which text do you think best answers the question in its title? Why? _____

_____

2. Which text do you think is more interesting? Why? _____

_____

3. Write a new title for each text. _____

_____

Word Partners

cause waste

cut down on waste

dangerous waste

get rid of waste

reduce waste

GO ONLINE
to practice
word partners ▶◀

4. What questions do you have for the writers about why we sleep and laugh? Write a question for each reading. _____

_____

● Make Connections: Text to World

A. Think about the two texts. Both writers use quoted speech. Complete the web with examples of quoted speech to show why each writer used it.

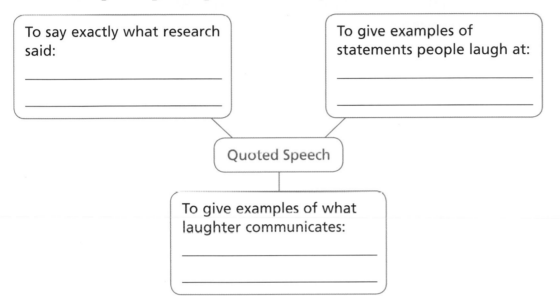

To say exactly what research said:
_____
_____

To give examples of statements people laugh at:
_____
_____

Quoted Speech

To give examples of what laughter communicates:
_____
_____

B. Read each situation. Think about the texts and then write an answer to each question. Look at the Oxford 2000 keywords on page 133 and find five words to help you.

1. Pedro stayed up all night studying for his test. He just arrived at class. For his test, he needs to write an essay to answer a question. He knows the information, but he can't think of what to write. Why?

_____

_____

2. Katia had a bad day at work. She doesn't feel good about her performance. She comes home and doesn't know what to do. She is feeling sad. She starts to read a book but then thinks about watching her favorite show. It's always funny. What should she do? Why?

_____

_____

Chant

GO ONLINE for the Chapter 3 Vocabulary & Grammar Chant

Look at the word bank for Unit 1. Check (✓) the words you know.
Circle the words you want to learn better.

OXFORD 2000 🔑			
Adjectives	**Nouns**		**Verbs**
awake	area	result	concentrate
enough	benefit (to)	sleep	control
funny	brain	system	dream
important	connection	task	identify
positive	experiment	test	remember
similar	humor	waste	repair
	joke		
	memory		
	model		
	muscle		
	reaction (to)		

PRACTICE WITH THE OXFORD 2000 🔑

A. Use the words in the chart. Match adjectives with nouns.

1. _____*funny joke*_____   2. _____

3. _____   4. _____

5. _____

B. Use the words in the chart. Match verbs with nouns.

1. _____*control a reaction*_____   2. _____

3. _____   4. _____

5. _____

C. Use the words in the chart. Match verbs with adjective noun partners.

1. _*identify a positive connection*_   2. _____

3. _____   4. _____

5. _____

UNIT 2 Individuals and Society

CHAPTER 4 A Business of One?

Reading 1: Who Is Self-Employed?
Reading 2: What Is Crowdfunding?

▲ **BEFORE READING**
- Oxford 2000 🔑 words to talk about business
- Notice spelling patterns for long vowels
- ◐ **Make connections: Text to self**

▲▲ **DURING READING**
- Word families • Understand bar graphs
- Adjective clauses after objects and subjects
- ◐ **Make connections: Text to text**

▲▲▲ **AFTER READING**
Summarizing and retelling
- ◐ **Make connections: Text to world**

CHAPTER 5 How Do We Fit In?

Reading 1: Why Is Fashion Important?
Reading 2: What Is Culture Shock?

▲ **BEFORE READING**
- Oxford 2000 🔑 words to talk about how we fit into society
- Spelling patterns for the different sounds of t and t with other letters
- ◐ **Make connections: Text to self**

▲▲ **DURING READING**
- Understand phrasal verbs • Make inferences
- Present, present progressive, and present perfect
- ◐ **Make connections: Text to text**

▲▲▲ **AFTER READING**
Summarizing and retelling
- ◐ **Make connections: Text to world**

CHAPTER 6 Making a Difference with Technology

Reading 1: A New Device Gives Hope
Reading 2: Helping the Deaf to Feel and See Sound

▲ **BEFORE READING**
- Oxford 2000 🔑 words to talk about how technology can help people • Spelling the /s/ sound with c
- ◐ **Make connections: Text to self**

▲▲ **DURING READING**
- Use negative prefixes • Recognize argument • Use could, should, and will have to to discuss possibility and argue a point
- ◐ **Make connections: Text to text**

▲▲▲ **AFTER READING**
Summarizing and retelling
- ◐ **Make connections: Text to world**

UNIT WRAP UP Making a Difference Extend Your Skills

- Notice spelling patterns for long vowels
- Word families
- Understand bar graphs
- Adjective clauses after objects and subjects

▲ BEFORE READING ▶ Oxford 2000 ✎ words to talk about business

Learn Vocabulary

A. Match each description to the correct picture.

1. When you **compete**, you try to win or to be better than someone else.

   Businesses compete for customers. They lower their prices and sometimes give free gifts.

2. When something **makes a difference**, it changes something. It has an effect.

   We planted a garden. It makes a difference. The area looks much nicer.

3. When you get the **message** across, you communicate your ideas well.

   Our new advertisement gets the message across. It says what we believe in.

4. When something is **available**, it's ready for you to use or have.

   There are many jobs available in the computer field.

B. Match each picture to the correct description.

__1__ I **earn** money by working at a very nice restaurant.

_____ The number of computer products **increases** each day.

_____ I have **Internet access** on my phone so I can read the news online and send emails.

_____ My job is **easy** to do from home. I use my laptop. I have everything I need here.

_____ I have **projects** to do at home. I need to fix the sink and paint the bathroom.

_____ There are many social **opportunities** on my college campus. You can join the student government, sports teams, and many other study groups and clubs.

1.
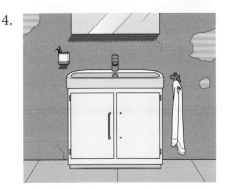

2.

3.

4.

5.

6.
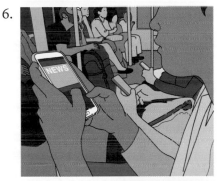

C. Complete the paragraph with the words and phrases from the box.

easy	increase	opportunities
~~Internet access~~	making a difference	project

People all over the world have _____Internet access_____. You can find

information, read articles, and communicate with anyone using it. There are so many

_____ now that we have the Internet. People can learn how to

do any _____. For example, it's

_____ to learn by watching a video. In addition, the number

of people with Internet access continues to _____. It's

_____ in our lives.

Oxford 2000 🔑

Use the Oxford 2000 list on page 133 to find more words to describe the pictures on these pages. Share your words with a partner.

GO ONLINE for more practice

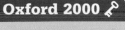

Preview the Text

D. Look at the text and bar graph on page 62. Answer the questions.

1. What is the title of the bar graph? _____

2. What do you think each bar on the graph shows? _____

3. What is the title of the text? _____

4. What do you think *self-employed* means? _____

5. The word *advantage* has a similar meaning to *benefit*. What do you think *disadvantage* means? _____

E. Look at the text on page 62. Circle the correct answer.

1. What will the text do?
   a. describe someone
   b. define something
   c. explain how to do something

3. These words are in the text. Which one does not have a similar meaning to *increase*?
   a. jump
   b. decrease
   c. rise

2. The text discusses advertising online. What do you think is an example of an online advertisement?
   a. a picture of a product on the Internet
   b. a message on a sign in a store
   c. a text message from your friend about a product

4. What do you think the phrase *run your own business* means?
   a. to work for someone's business
   b. to be a runner
   c. to be the manager of your business

Sounds of English

Spelling Connection

A. Listen to the word *rain*. Do you hear the long a, /eɪ/? Often, a vowel will be long if it is followed by another vowel, like in *rain*. Look at this chart and listen to the words to help you connect each spelling pattern with a long vowel sound.

vowel followed by another vowel	*rain, beat, coat, read, lie, due*
vowel followed by the letter *y*	*say, day, key*
vowel-consonant-e	*date, hole, mile, rule*

B. Listen to the words. Underline the letters that make a long vowel sound in each word.

available   easily   increase

C. These words are in the text on page 62. Underline the letters that make a long vowel sound.

between   cases   pay   people   places   states

⬤ **Make Connections:** Text to Self

A. Answer the questions.

1. Self-employed people don't work for someone else; they work on their own. If you were self-employed, what would you do to earn money? _____

   _____

2. Do you think the number of people who are self-employed is increasing? Why or why not? _____

   _____

3. List three jobs you think many self-employed people do. _____

   _____

4. List three areas of the world that you think have many self-employed people. _____

   _____

5. What benefits are there to being self-employed? List three. _____

   _____

B. Why do you think people become self-employed? Think about the hours, places, and types of jobs people work. Complete the web.

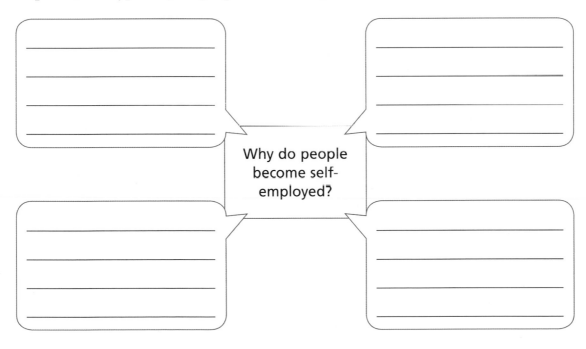

◉ Reading 1

A. The writer uses phrases to discuss years and other numbers in the text. Skim the text and read the phrases. What numbers do they include?

Who Is Self-Employed?

In many places in the world, the number of people who are self-employed is **increasing**. A self-employed person is someone who works for himself or herself and not for another business or organization. In countries like the United States, the number of people who are self-employed has been increasing since 1970 but had its biggest jump after 2000. There was a 42 percent increase. What can explain this increase in the number of workers who are creating and running their own businesses? First, there has been a decrease in jobs **available**. Between 2000 and 2012, businesses with 100 or more employees lost 2.3 million jobs. A lot of people had to find work. Some started their own businesses. Second, more people have **Internet access**. It's **easy** for people to share their ideas with the world on the Internet. They can sell products and advertise online. In addition, people **compete** to create better products at lower prices. All of this competition encourages creativity.

Many people do business on the Internet. They buy and sell products, but being self-employed is different. It means that you are not working another job. You **earn** most of your money from your business. One global organization defines self-employed people as those who work 30 or more hours a week for themselves.

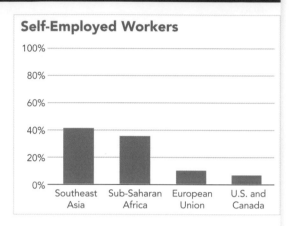

Self-Employed Workers

Research shows that self-employed people work more hours, get paid less, and worry more than others. Yet the numbers of self-employed continue to rise. Why? One word: happiness. Despite the disadvantage, there is one big advantage. You manage your time and your work. And this is a great **opportunity**. Yet not all the self-employed are happy. Some people are self-employed because there are no other jobs available. In fact, some areas with the highest number of self-employed people are also the poorest areas of the world (like Southeast Asia and Sub-Saharan Africa). People there don't have other job opportunities. Self-employed people live in different places all over the world. They have different jobs and experiences. However, one thing is the same: The numbers of self-employed people are increasing, and so are the products they create.

Stop and Think

Why does competition encourage creativity?

B. Now read the text and focus on the phrases that include numbers. Check your understanding.

Check Your Understanding

C. Match each answer to the correct question.

1. __b__ Why do some of the poorest places have high numbers of self-employed people?

2. _____ Why is Internet access important to being self-employed?

3. _____ What is a disadvantage of being self-employed?

4. _____ What is a main advantage of being self-employed?

a. You work longer hours and worry more.

b. ~~There are no other opportunities.~~

c. It is easy to let people know about your product.

d. You manage your time.

Vocabulary Strategy

Word Families

Some words are in the same family. Learning word families can help you increase your vocabulary quickly. The words in a word family are different parts of speech, but their meanings are similar. Often, the word form has a suffix that shows its part of speech.

Noun	Verb	Adjective
availability		available
competition / competitor*	compete	competitive
creativity / creator*	create	creative
earnings / earner*	earn	
employment / employer*	employ	employed
organization / organizer*	organize	organizational

The endings -or and -er on competitor, creator, earner, employer, organizer, and other words refer to a person.

GO ONLINE
for more
practice

D. Write the correct word from the chart in the Vocabulary Strategy box to complete each sentence.

1. The biggest ____employer____ in my city is a well-known bank. More than 25,000 people work there.

2. As a server, I _____ close to $150 a day.

3. I work with a lot of _____ people at the art museum.

4. I'm _____ to meet between 5 and 8 tonight.

Understand Bar Graphs

Writers use graphs to show numerical information like money amounts, years, and other items that can be measured with numbers. It's important to know how to read bar graphs to understand many types of texts. Look at the bar graph on page 62. The title "Self-Employed Workers" explains what the graph shows. The label "Percentage of the Workforce" shows what each bar is. The *y*-axis is the vertical axis (up and down). It shows the percentages from 0 to 100 percent. The *x*-axis is the horizontal axis (left and right). It lists the names of different areas in the world. To read the bar graph, look at the bar above each area on the *x*-axis. Read the *y*-axis to see the percentage of self-employed people in that area.

GO ONLINE for more practice

E. Look at the bar graph on page 62. Circle the correct answer.

1. Which area has the most self-employed workers?

    a. Southeast Asia   b. Sub-Saharan Africa   c. European Union

2. Which area has the fewest self-employed workers?

    a. Sub-Saharan Africa   b. European Union   c. U.S. and Canada

3. In which area are more than 40 percent of people self-employed?

    a. Southeast Asia   b. Sub-Saharan Africa   c. U.S. and Canada

◉ Reading 2

A. Listen and read along.

What Is Crowdfunding?

More and more people are using crowdfunding to pay for their **projects** and create new products. Crowdfunding is when a person or business gets many small payments from a large number of people. Usually, the way to do this is to use the Internet. Instead of trying to get a few people to give thousands of dollars, you get hundreds of people, maybe thousands, to give a few dollars. But this is still not **easy**. You want people to see the value of your idea. How will you get them to give the dollars they **earn** to you?

There are websites that make this **opportunity** possible. Kickstarter and GoGetFunding are popular. You create a

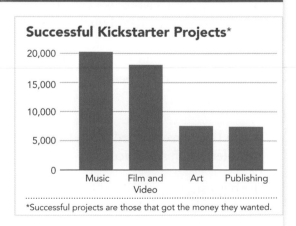

Successful Kickstarter Projects*

*Successful projects are those that got the money they wanted.

short video to explain your project. The most important part is getting your **message** across. Just because you've made your idea known doesn't mean you will get the money you need. You still need to sell your idea.

Stop and Think

The value of a dime is ten cents. What does value mean in this sentence: "You want people to see the value of your idea"?

Many people begin by explaining what the product is and then telling why people need it. For example, one of the most popular crowdfunded products is a watch. The Pebble watch connects with information on a smartphone that will send information to the watch. More than 65,000 people gave money for this product. Crowdfunding raised $10.3 million for it. However, it's not just products that people use crowdfunding for. People use it for their music, film, art, or writing projects.

Projects usually get from 25 to 40 percent of their money from crowdfunding sites. Who is giving all the money? When people need money, they often ask their friends and family. Crowdfunding often works the same way, but once you create your video and message, your friends share it with their friends. If you've created a message that people can connect to, you get many more people to give. Why do these people give? First, there is the "feel-good" factor. Giving money makes people feel good. Second, many small businesses offer rewards to people. Third, sometimes the reward is simply getting to use the product. And this is part of the success of crowdfunding. You could make a **difference**.

Grammar in the Readings

Notice adjective clauses after objects and subjects in the readings.

Writers use adjective clauses to add information about a noun. Use *that* for objects, things, or places.

       object noun   **adjective clause**

*There are <u>websites</u> **that** make this opportunity possible.*

Use *who* for people.

              object noun   **adjective clause**

*A self-employed person is <u>someone</u> **who** works for himself or herself.*

Writers also use adjective clauses after subject nouns to help define the noun.

    subject noun   **adjective clause**

*The <u>number</u> of people **who** are self-employed is increasing.*

GO ONLINE
for grammar
practice

Check Your Understanding

B. Answer the questions.

1. Why do people use crowdfunding to earn money for their projects? _____

_____

2. What do people describe in their project message? _____

_____

3. Summarize the reasons why people give their money to crowdfunding projects.

_____

Vocabulary Strategy: Word Families

C. Complete the chart.

Nouns	Verbs	Adjective	Adverb
_____	need		
_____	pay		
		_____	easily
explanation	_____		
identification	_____		
		usual	_____

D. Complete each sentence with a word from the chart in Activity C.

1. It's not _____ to find a good job. There is a lot of competition.

2. One _____ for why many people use crowdfunding is you can get a lot of people involved.

3. I _____ don't give money to people I don't know.

4. Many people _____ opportunities to share their message.

5. I could not _____ which project I liked better.

Reading Strategy: Understand Bar Graphs

E. Look at the bar graph on page 64. Circle the correct answer.

1. What sentence in the text does the bar graph support?

   a. More than 65,000 people gave money for this product.

   b. Giving money to something you believe in makes people feel good.

   c. People use it for their music, film, art, or writing projects.

2. Which project type is the most successful?

   a. music   b. film and video   c. art

3. Which project type is the least successful?

   a. music   b. film and video   c. publishing

4. Which project types have more than 15,000 successful projects?

   a. music and art   b. film and video and publishing   c. music and film and video

● Make Connections: Text to Text

A. Both texts define an important word or phrase. Write the word or phrase and the definition in the chart below.

	Word or Phrase		Definition
Reading 1	→ _____	→	_____
Reading 2	→ _____	→	_____

B. Both writers use numbers. Look at the phrases that describe numbers. Cross out the number that does not belong.

1. **Between 2000 and 2012**, businesses with 100 or more employees lost 2.3 million jobs.

   2005   2014   2011

2. On a popular website that allows people to sell their products, there are **more than 180,000** results for smart phone cases.

   180,019   179,999   181,000

3. Projects usually get **from 25 to 40** percent of their money from crowdfunding sites.

   20 percent   27 percent   40 percent

4. **More than 65,000** people gave money for this product.

   66,000   65,000   65,433

5. One global organization defines self-employed as those who work **30 or more hours** a week for themselves.

   30   60   20

C. Both writers use signal words. Answer the questions by completing the rest of the sentence.

1. What can explain the increase in workers who are creating and running their own businesses?

   a. First, _____

   b. Second, _____

2. Why do people give money to crowdfunding projects?

   a. First, _____

   b. Second, _____

   c. Third, _____

Summarizing and Retelling

A. Complete the sentences with the words from the box. Then read the paragraphs to a partner to summarize.

Adjectives	Nouns	Verbs
available easy	difference Internet message opportunity project	compete earn increase

1.   In the first text, the topic is self-employed workers. The writer explains why more

people are becoming self-employed. There were not enough jobs

_____ , so people started their own businesses. Many people have

_____ access. This makes it _____ to share their

ideas. People _____ to create better products, and more products are

available. Not everyone who is self-employed is happy. In some countries, there are no

other opportunities to _____ money. But the number of people who

are self-employed continues to _____ .

2.   In the second text, the writer talks about crowdfunding. It's a(n)

_____ to get many people to give money for an idea you have. The

writer discusses how to make a(n) _____ successful. One thing is to

get your _____ across so people want to give money to your project.

Another thing that makes crowdfunding popular is people feel that they can make a(n)

_____ .

B. Both writers use adjective clauses. Complete each sentence with an adjective clause. Use the information in parentheses in your clause with *who* or *that*.

1. The Internet makes a difference for people __who are self-employed__ . (are self-employed)

2. The Internet also gives people _____ business opportunities. (use crowdfunding)

Word Partners

little opportunity

wonderful
opportunity

get an opportunity

miss the opportunity

opportunity for

_____

GO ONLINE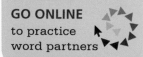
to practice
word partners

3. There are high numbers of people _____ in poor areas of the world. (are self-employed)

4. Projects _____ get the message across in their video. (are successful)

Make Connections: Text to World

A. Think about the two texts. Check the statements you agree with.

1. _____ Being self-employed is better than working for someone else.

2. _____ Being self-employed is easy.

3. _____ There are many benefits to self-employment.

4. _____ Crowdfunding is for creative people.

5. _____ Crowdfunding is a great way to get people to give money.

6. _____ It's better to buy products at the store than to give money to a crowdfunding project.

B. Think about texts that define ideas. Answer the questions.

1. Why do writers use bar graphs? _____

_____

_____

2. How do signal words help the reader? _____

_____

_____

3. When do writers include definitions in the text? _____

_____

_____

4. What words and phrases do writers use to describe numbers? _____

_____

_____

C. Discuss your answers from Activities A and B with a partner. Share opinions and examples. Look at the Oxford 2000 keywords on page 133 and find five words to help you.

Chant

GO ONLINE for the Chapter 4 Vocabulary & Grammar Chant

How Do We Fit In?

- Spelling patterns for the different sounds of *t* and *t* with other letters
- Understand phrasal verbs
- Make inferences
- Present, present progressive, and present perfect

▲ **BEFORE READING** ▶ Oxford 2000 ⚿ words to talk about how we fit into society

Learn Vocabulary

A. Match each picture to the correct description.

_____ A **tradition** is something that people in a specific place have done or believed for a long time.

It's a tradition to drink tea in the afternoon in England.

___1___ Your **values** are your thoughts about what is wrong and right.

I share many of the same values as my parents about money. We save our money.

_____ **Society** is a large group of people who live in the same area and have the same ideas about how to live.

In many societies, children begin school around age five.

_____ To **fit in** is to be able to live in an easy and natural way with other people.

I fit in with my brother's friends. They like playing soccer too.

1.

2.

3.

4.

B. Match each sentence to the correct picture.

1. A popular **fashion trend** is to wear jeans.

2. It's **human nature** to laugh when others do.

3. In my **culture**, everyone learns to eat with chopsticks.

4. I feel **lonely** at my new school.

Oxford 2000 🔑

Use the Oxford 2000 list on page 133 to find more words to describe the pictures on these pages. Share your words with a partner.

GO ONLINE
for more practice

C. When you *follow* someone or something, you do what someone or something says you should do. Write each collocation under the correct picture.

| follow a fashion trend | follow directions | follow traffic signs |

1. _____   2. _____   3. _____

Preview the Text

D. Look at the photos on page 74. Answer the questions. Use the bold words from pages 70–71.

1. What does the top photo show? _____

_____

2. What does the bottom photo show? _____

_____

3. What do you learn from looking at the two photos? _____

_____

E. Circle the best answer.

1. What will the text do?

   a. give directions to follow

   b. explain why people do something

   c. describe an event that happened

2. The first sentence of the text is "Fashion is everywhere, in homes, in architecture, but especially in clothing." What word will the writer discuss more?

   a. clothing

   b. architecture

   c. homes

3. The first sentence of the second paragraph is "To try on clothes is to try on another identity, to be someone different." Which word or phrase has the meaning *who or what someone is*?

   a. identity

   b. clothes

   c. try on

4. The first sentence of the third paragraph uses the phrase *developments in society*. What do you think is an example of a development in society?

   a. You buy a new shirt.

   b. Clothing stores also begin to sell products online.

   c. Your friend designs clothing.

Sounds of English

Spelling Connection

🔊 A. Listen to the different sounds the *t* makes in the words below.

    fit   tradition   nature   clothing

Notice the spelling pattern. Listen for /t/ in *fit*, the /ʃ/ in *tradition*, the /tʃ/ in *nature*, and the /ð / in *clothing*. Note that *th* can also make the unvoiced /θ/ sound as in *think*. Use a dictionary to help you know when to use /ð/ or /θ/.

B. The following words are in the texts on pages 74 and 76–77. Write them in the correct column. Some words may belong in more than one column.

| action | architecture | particular | population | they |
| shirt | society | that | this | culture |

/t/ in *fit*	/ʃ/ in *tradition*	/tʃ/ in *nature*	/ð/ in *clothing*

● Make Connections: Text to Self

A. Think about fashion. Complete the chart.

Questions	Your Answer
1. What is a popular fashion trend now?	
2. Do you follow fashion trends? Why or why not?	
3. What can you learn about someone from the clothes he or she wears?	
4. Do students and businesspeople wear similar clothes? Why or why not?	
5. What causes changes in fashion?	

B. Complete the web. List some of the things that affect fashion.

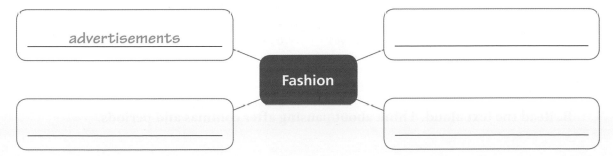

advertisements

Fashion

◀)) **Reading 1**

A. Use punctuation to help you read phrases. Give a short pause after a comma. Then go on to the next phrase. A period is used after a complete sentence or thought. Pause for a little longer between sentences. Listen to the text and focus on the pauses after commas and periods.

Why Is Fashion Important?

Stop and Think

What values does your fashion show?

By the 20th century, most people no longer wore handmade clothing. Fashion had changed. They dressed more simply and bought their clothes from stores.

Fashion is everywhere, in homes, in architecture, but especially in clothing. Ask yourself why you are wearing a particular color, length of pants, or design. Is it because you saw an advertisement or someone wearing something similar? Not everyone likes to say they **follow** fashion **trends**. However, it's **human nature** to want to **fit in**. Imagine walking into a room of people. Who do you talk to? Many people talk to the person wearing clothes like theirs. Some choose the person whose clothes they like. Whichever you choose, it is connected to human needs. The first and most important human needs are water and food, the things the body needs. The second most important are connected to feeling safe. The third is our deep need to **belong**. Fashion fits in with this need. Walk down the street and look at the clothes people wear. The clothes show who they are. They show the group the person connects with. Is it a businessman in a business suit or a student in a T-shirt and jeans? You can learn a lot about a person from his or her clothes. What do each of these people do? What do they value?

To try on clothes is to try on another identity, to be someone different. With our clothing, we tell the world about ourselves and the groups we identify with. Everyone follows fashion. Even if you don't follow fashion trends, what you choose to wear shows your **values**. What fashions are we following? Fashion is connected to **culture**. There are groups who have worn the same styles for hundreds of years. These people follow the **traditions** of the past. Other people try out new designs.

Often, developments in **society** change fashion. In the 18th century, wealthy men wore bright colors of silk and velvet. However, in the 20th century, they wore more standard, plain clothing. It was the fashion of business. Designers made these clothes so men could move and work easily. Fashion also is connected to society. As society changes, fashion changes too. For instance, most people no longer have their clothes individually made for them. Due to this, we all buy clothing from many of the same stores. This doesn't mean we don't have choices. Walk down the street of any big city and you'll see something new. But even if it's new, it fits in with a group or belief. That's why we choose to wear it. We want to be accepted in that group. We want to be seen as young, rich, or smart. Fashion will continue to change as society does. And what we wear will too because as humans we have a deep need to belong.

B. Read the text aloud. Think about pausing after commas and periods.

Check Your Understanding

C. Write _T_ (true) or _F_ (false). Rewrite false statements to be true.

1. __F__ Following fashion is not connected to fitting in.

Following fashion is connected to fitting in. _____

2. _____ The need to belong is the most important human need.

_____

3. _____ The clothes you wear show the group you belong to.

_____

4. _____ Changes in society and business affect fashion.

_____

Vocabulary Strategy

Understand Phrasal Verbs

Some verbs in English are phrases. They include a verb and a preposition.

verb   preposition

It's human nature to want to **fit in**.

The meaning of the phrasal verb is different from the individual words. Most phrasal verbs can be replaced by another verb that means the same thing. _Fit in_ means "belong."

Phrasal verbs are used often in English, so it's good to know their meanings. Follow these steps to help you.

1. Read the sentence and identify a verb + preposition. Note that not all verbs and prepositions are phrasal verbs. For example, in "I walked into the room," _walked into_ is not a phrasal verb—_into the room_ tells where the person walked.

2. Look for a verb + preposition that has a different meaning from the verb. Think of another verb that could be used in the phrasal verb's place.

GO ONLINE
for more
practice

D. Underline the phrasal verb in each sentence.

1. With our clothing, we tell the world about ourselves and the groups we <u>identify with</u>.

2. To try on clothes is to try on another identity, to be someone different.

3. Other people try out new things.

4. Can you figure out why fashion changes?

5. Did you pick out a new coat yet?

Make Inferences

Readers make inferences to help connect what they are reading to what they know. Making an inference can help you better understand the writer's ideas.

1. Read a sentence or group of sentences.

2. Think about why the writer included this information. What is the writer saying? What can you learn?

3. Make an inference to help you understand the writer's idea. Think of what you know and how it connects to the text.

   Not everyone likes to say they follow fashion trends, but it's human nature to want to fit in.

   Question: *Why don't people want to say they follow fashion trends?*

   Inference: *I think the writer is saying that people like to be seen as different.*

GO ONLINE
for more
practice

E. Match each question to an inference based on the text on page 74.

Questions

1. __c__ Why do some people try out new designs?

2. _____ Why do people wear different clothes to different places?

3. _____ Why do people wear styles from the past?

4. _____ Why is trying on clothes like trying on a new identity?

Inferences

a. People want to be accepted where they go. They change their clothes so they fit in.

b. People look at your clothes and form an idea of what group you belong to. This might change your idea of yourself.

c. ~~People want to show that they are creative and they like change.~~

d. People want to show they value traditions.

◉ Reading 2

A. Read the text on your own.

What Is Culture Shock?

According to the United Nations Population Fund, in 2013, 232 million people, 3.2 percent of the world's population, lived outside their home country. In 2009, the United States and the United Kingdom were the most popular places to move to. However, people also leave these places. In 2013, the United Kingdom lost 400 citizens a day. Many of these people were college educated and looking for other job and social opportunities. There's a phrase for the effect making your home in another **society** and **culture** has on you: *culture shock*. A shock is a bad surprise, but that's not actually how most people experience culture shock. Culture shock is when someone feels he or she doesn't **belong** in a new country. First, most people feel excitement at being in a new place: There are opportunities and possibilities. However, the second stage is different. People now notice how the new place is different from home. Everyday things like ordering food in a restaurant, shopping, and using the train are different. These small things can seem big. People get upset. It's **human nature**. They compare their new place to home. They think of home as better. When you know how to do things, like communicate in the language, it's easier. At this point, many people feel **lonely**. And feeling lonely can affect how you communicate with others. Lonely people often see other people as a danger. They don't trust them. As a result, they don't talk to others. There are people all around them, but they feel that they don't belong.

A university website gives tips for people to **follow** to help with culture shock:

(1) Do not think things will be like they are at home. How people do business and communicate and what times of day they eat are often different. (2) Talk to people. Show you want to learn about them and their culture. (3) Do not let one person's actions affect your idea of the whole society. (4) Understand that everyday things, such as how close people stand to one another, how people wait in line, and how long people pause in conversations, are different. For example, during conversations, most Americans do not let much time pass before they feel the need to start speaking. Other cultures are much more comfortable with pauses in conversation. People in different cultures have different **values**. Try to notice these things and understand the new culture you are in. You may want to connect with others from home. While it can be helpful to be with people from your country, try to identify with others. This doesn't mean you have to change who you are to **fit in**. Think about what you can share and what you can learn. If you concentrate on these things, then you can begin to feel less lonely. Maybe you are different, but you can be different and also belong.

Stop and Think
What other differences are there between cultures?

Grammar in the Readings

Notice the present, present progressive, and present perfect in the readings.

Writers use present tense to talk about things that are true now.

*Fashion **is** everywhere, in homes, in architecture, but especially in clothing.*

Writers use the present progressive to describe something that is happening.

*Ask yourself why you **are wearing** a particular color, length of pants, or design.*

Writers use the present perfect to talk about something that happened in the past and is still happening.

*There are groups who **have worn** the same styles for hundreds of years.*

GO ONLINE
for grammar practice

Check Your Understanding

B. Complete the sentences to summarize the text on pages 76–77.

1. There are two stages of culture shock. In the first, people feel _____ .

   In the second, people get _____ . They feel _____ .

2. There are four tips to help people with culture shock.

   a. Do not think that things _____ .

   b. Communicate with others and _____ .

   c. Do not let an individual's behavior _____ .

   d. Know that many things _____ .

3. The writer says that it can be good to _____ but

   _____ .

Recycle

the Vocabulary
Strategy

Vocabulary Strategy: Understand Phrasal Verbs

C. Underline the phrasal verb in each sentence, and match it to a verb with a similar meaning.

1. __*a*__ Many people <u>look for</u> new job opportunities in other countries.

2. _____ Can you hang on a minute? I have to answer the phone.

3. _____ Don't give up. Living somewhere new is hard, but you can do it.

a. seek

b. quit

c. wait

Recycle

the Reading
Strategy

Reading Strategy: Make Inferences

D. Match each question to an inference based on the text on pages 76–77.

1. __*b*__ Why do people feel they don't belong in a new culture?

2. _____ Why isn't it good to let one person's actions affect your idea of a society?

3. _____ How does showing you want to learn about a new culture help you?

4. _____ What does the writer mean by "they don't trust them"?

Inferences

a. A society is more than just one person.

b. ~~They don't make connections with the people there. They feel they are not part of the group.~~

c. You concentrate on new things and not just your feelings.

d. People believe that others are not good people.

⬤ Make Connections: Text to Text

A. Both texts discuss human nature and fitting into society. Answer the questions. Look at the texts on pages 74 and 76–77 to help you.

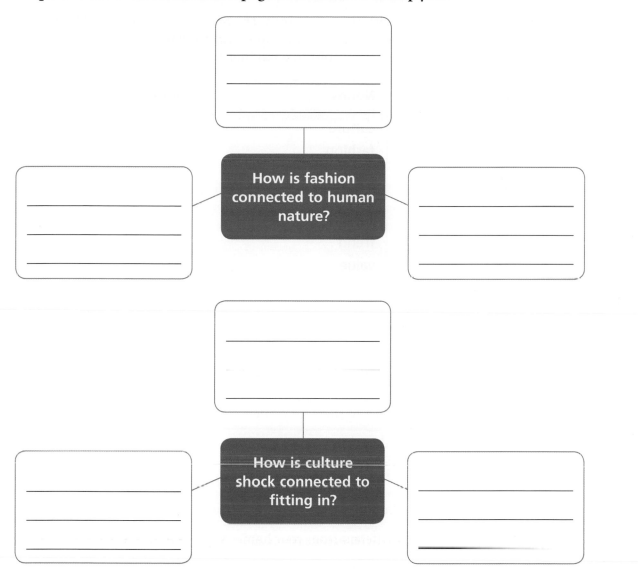

B. The writers organize the texts in different ways. Read each description. Write
_1_ if it matches Reading 1 and _2_ if it matches Reading 2.

1. _____ uses a numbered list

2. _____ defines a key word

3. _____ asks questions to connect to the reader

4. _____ gives statistics

5. _____ gives examples from history

6. _____ uses an _if-then_ statement to show cause and effect

7. _____ ends with a prediction for the future

8. _____ purpose is to change the readers' behavior or actions

Summarizing and Retelling

A. Complete the sentences with the words from the box. Some of the words have to be changed to fit the sentences. For example, *tradition* has to be changed to *traditions*. Then read the paragraphs to a partner to retell the ideas.

Adjectives	Nouns	Verbs
human	culture	belong
lonely	fashion	fit
	nature	follow
	society	
	tradition	
	trend	
	value	

1.   Some things are part of _____ _____. This means that everyone does or experiences these things. One of those things is the deep need to belong. We wear clothes to show the group we _____ in with. Sometimes people wear clothes to show they value _____ from the past. Other times people follow the newest _____ if they care about _____.

2.   Many people experience _____ shock. This is when _____ is different from your home. Many people feel _____ in this situation. But there are tips you can _____. Understand that people have different _____. Focus on what you can learn about the culture. You may be different, but you still _____.

B. Use the words from the chart in Activity A to discuss the topics below with a partner.

1. Talk about a fashion trend. Why do you think it happened? Why do you think people follow it? Why do you like or not like it?

2. Talk about culture shock. How might people act when they have culture shock? What other tips could help them?

Word Partners

member of society

the rest of society

modern society

wider society

fit into society

GO ONLINE
to practice
word partners

Make Connections: Text to World

A. Do you agree or disagree with the writers? Check the statements you agree with, and then discuss your ideas with a partner.

1. _____ The clothes you wear show who you are.

2. _____ Fashion is important to people because they want to belong to a group.

3. _____ No one's clothes are really different. They fit into an idea or group in society.

4. _____ Learning about a culture can help you feel better.

5. _____ You can be different and still fit in.

B. Think about the two texts. Complete the chart to make predictions.

Now	In the Year 2065 (Future)
1. People wear _____ .	1. People will wear _____ .
2. _____ is having an effect on fashion.	2. _____ will affect fashion.
3. In 2013, 3.2 percent of the world's population lived outside their home country.	3. In 2050, _____ percent of the world's population will live outside their home country.
4. Many people leave home to move to the United States or Great Britain.	4. People will leave home to move to _____ and _____ .

C. Both texts discuss ideas that are connected to a person's identity. What other things affect how you think about yourself? Complete the web with your own ideas. Look at the Oxford 2000 keywords on page 133 and find five words to help you.

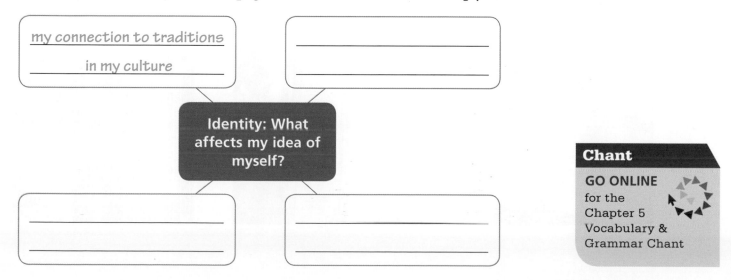

my connection to traditions in my culture

Identity: What affects my idea of myself?

Chant

GO ONLINE
for the
Chapter 5
Vocabulary &
Grammar Chant

Making a Difference with Technology

- Spelling the /s/ sound with *c*
- Use negative prefixes
- Recognize argument

- Use *could, should,* and *will have to* to discuss possibility and argue a point

▲ BEFORE READING ▶ Oxford 2000 ✎ words to talk about how technology can help people

Learn Vocabulary

A. Match each picture to the correct description.

_____ The doctor has to **operate** on my brother. He had a problem with his heart.

_____ Now there are **devices** that let you talk on the phone without using your hands.

_____ I felt the ground **shake** when the truck came close by.

_____ I wanted to buy my mom the beautiful sweater, but it was too **expensive**.

___1___ I couldn't **hear** my friend talk. The restaurant was too loud.

_____ I was not **able** to walk after my car accident.

1.

2.

3.

4.
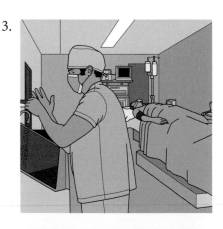

5.

6.

B. Match each description to the correct picture.

1. Technology is so **advanced**. Smartphones can now do what many computers do.

2. My **permanent** home is in Madrid. I am only in New York for a few months.

3. I can't **afford** to buy a ticket to Tokyo. The airline prices are too high.

4. I have **hope** that my mom will get better. She is very sick, but she is strong.

C. Complete the paragraph with the words from the box.

| able to | advanced | ~~devices~~ | hear | hope | permanent |

It is not safe for people to talk on the phone while driving. Because of this,

businesses have created new _____devices_____ so people are

_____ talk on the phone without using their hands. This is one

example of _____ technology. However, this is not a(n)

_____ way to make driving safer. People talking on the phone while

driving sometimes don't _____ other cars and sounds. They

concentrate on their phone call and not the road, and accidents still happen. In the

future, cars will not have drivers. The _____ is that this will make

driving safer for everyone.

Oxford 2000 🔑

Use the Oxford 2000 list on page 133 to find more words to describe the pictures on these pages. Share your words with a partner.

GO ONLINE for more practice

Preview the Text

D. Answer the questions.

1. Look at the photo and read the caption at the bottom of page 86. What do you think a prosthetic limb is?

_____

_____

2. *Medical* means "connected with medicine, hospitals, or doctors." Look at the collocations with *medical*. Discuss what they mean with a partner. Use a dictionary if needed.

   medical development　*medical center*　*medical condition*

E. Look at the text on page 86. Circle the best answer.

1. What do you think the writer will do?

   a. explain how to do something

   b. tell why something is important

   c. tell about a famous person

3. Who do you think Les Baugh is?

   a. a doctor

   b. the writer

   c. a person without arms

2. What do you think the topic of the text is?

   a. how medical workers and scientists work

   b. how people lose their limbs

   c. how we can help people who have lost limbs

Sounds of English

Spelling Connection

🔊 A. The /s/ sound is often spelled with an *s*, but it can be spelled with a *c*. Most often when *c* is followed by consonants or the vowels *a, o,* or *u,* the *c* makes the /k/ sound. However, if the c is followed by the letter *y* or the vowels *e* or *i,* it can make the /s/ sound. The letters *sc* together also make the /s/ sound as in *muscle.* Listen to the words in the chart below.

/s/ Spelled with *c*	/k/ Spelled with *c*
city　cycle　concentrate	can　click　concentrate　culture

🔊 B. Listen to the words. Circle the words that have an /s/ sound spelled with a *c* or an *s*. Underline the spelling pattern.

   advanced　　device　　expensive　　operate　　shake

C. These words are in the text on page 86. Circle the words that have an /s/ sound spelled with a *c*. Underline the words that have a /k/ sound spelled with a *c*.

   controlled　　doctors　　medical　　racing　　receive

● Make Connections: Text to Self

A. Answer the questions. Look at the Oxford 2000 keywords on page 133 and find words to help you.

1. If you could not use your arms, what would you use? _____

_____

2. What technology is available for people who don't have arms or legs? _____

_____

3. Is it easy for people without legs or arms to get around your city? Why or why not?

_____

_____

B. Think about how society can help people who don't have or can't use their arms or legs. Complete the web. Use a dictionary for help.

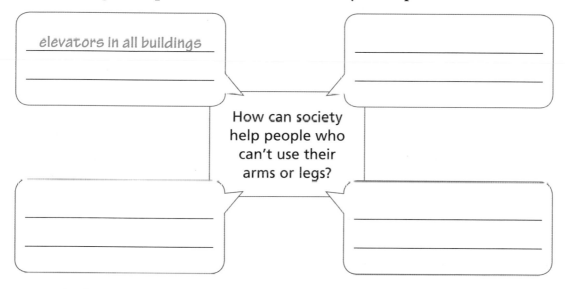

elevators in all buildings

How can society help people who can't use their arms or legs?

C. Check the statements you agree with. Then discuss your answers with a partner.

1. _____ If you lose your legs, it's permanent. You cannot walk again.

2. _____ People without a leg or arm can do most things that people with arms or legs can.

3. _____ It is difficult for people without a leg or arm to live in society.

4. _____ Most cities and buildings make it easy for people who have lost a leg or arm to get around.

5. _____ There are devices that are not expensive to help people without legs or arms.

◉ Reading 1

A. Words like *but*, *yet*, and *however* are used to contrast ideas. These words show ideas that are different. Listen to the text. Focus on how the contrast words are said. There is more stress on them.

A New Device Gives Hope

Power lines carry electricity to homes so your lights, TV, and other devices work.

Stop and Think

Nerves in Mr. Baugh's shoulder send and receive signals from his brain. Where else do we have nerves?

Les Baugh goes to a medical center like this one to practice using a prosthetic limb.

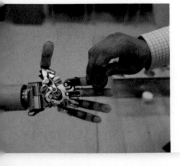

Les Baugh was like other boys his age. He liked to have fun. One day, he was racing his brother to the top of a hill. He got there first, but he ran into a power line and the electricity went through his body. He lost both of his arms. Doctors told him he would not live past 21. He is 59 now, and he has gone through most of his life without arms. Since he was 17, he has used his mouth to hold objects, to cook, to do all the other things we use our hands for. However, medical developments are changing this. A new prosthetic limb, which is a robotic arm and hand, allows Mr. Baugh to hold, pick up, and move objects. The prosthetic limb is controlled by his brain. Doctors attached it to Mr. Baugh's shoulder where his arm used to be. Mr. Baugh still has nerves, which send and receive messages from the brain, in his shoulder. Doctors connected the **device** to those nerves. Now, Mr. Baugh can move the prosthetic arm and hand. He simply thinks "close hand" or "lift arm," and the prosthetic moves. Devices like these are changing the lives of people who have lost arms, legs, and hands. Yet more research and development are needed.

Medical centers ask people like Mr. Baugh to try out the new devices. Then they make changes to make the devices better. If these devices allow people to do things they never thought possible, why aren't the devices for sale? There are several reasons. First, the devices have to meet safety rules before businesses can sell them. As a result, we need more testing. Second, scientists developed these devices to be very **advanced**. Prosthetics like the one Mr. Baugh was using have 100 different sensors. Sensors allow people to sense, or feel, objects. However, because these prosthetics are so advanced, they are very **expensive**, about $500,000. Because of this, scientists will have to make changes so that more people can **afford** them. The devices won't be as advanced, but they will cost less. Third, scientists should concentrate on creating prosthetics that are safe and easy to attach. For instance, doctors had to **operate** on Mr. Baugh so they could find the nerves where his arms once were. However, in the future, scientists think people will be **able to** control the prosthetics by a device they wear on their head. It will send signals from the person's brain to the prosthetic. More time and money are needed to make this possible. These devices are still being tested, but with today's advanced technology, many medical conditions are no longer **permanent**. People who once thought they would never be able to walk or hold a baby now have **hope**.

B. Read the text on your own. Stress the contrast words. Then ask yourself what the different ideas are.

Check Your Understanding

C. Answer the questions.

1. Explain how a prosthetic limb works. _____

_____

2. How old is Mr. Baugh now? _____

3. Where does Mr. Baugh use the prosthetic limb? _____

4. What do nerves do? _____

_____

5. Summarize why prosthetic limbs are not available to everyone. _____

_____

GO ONLINE
for more
practice

Vocabulary Strategy

Use Negative Prefixes

A prefix is a group of letters you add to the beginning of a word to change its meaning.

*I am able to walk. I am **un**able to walk.*

The prefix *un-* means "not." *Unable* means "not able."

The prefixes below also mean "not." They attach to some words.

dis- il- im- in- ir- non- un-

Many of the prefixes attach to adjectives, such as *able*. However, some also attach to nouns (*advantage/**dis**advantage*) and verbs (*agree/**dis**agree*).

D. Look at each word with a negative prefix. Write the meaning of the word and then list an example to show its meaning.

Word with Negative Prefix	Meaning	Example
1. <u>un</u>able*	not able	Les Baugh is unable to buy the prosthetic.
2. <u>im</u>possible		
3. <u>in</u>expensive		
4. <u>un</u>safe		
5. <u>im</u>permanent		

*The prefix *dis-* also connects to *able* forming the adjective *disabled*. We use this word to describe people who are not able to use a part of their body well.

Recognize Argument

In some texts, writers want you to think like them. They argue an idea. This is the purpose of the text. Identify arguments in these ways.

1. Ask why the writer is writing the text. Does the writer want you to think or do something?

2. Look at the verbs the writer uses. Do they use *should* or *will have to*? Do they tell the reader what needs to happen?

3. Look for examples. What do they support? How do they make the reader feel?

4. Look for words that signal cause and effect: *as a result, because, if/then.*

5. Look at the pronouns the writer uses. Writers may use *you* to talk to the reader or *we* to include the reader.

GO ONLINE
for more
practice

E. Read each statement from the text on page 86. Then answer the question to identify the writer's argument.

1. Devices like these are changing the lives of people who have lost arms, legs, and hands. What does the writer argue is needed? _____

2. Devices have to meet safety rules before businesses can sell them. What does the writer argue is needed? _____

3. Because these prosthetics are so advanced, they are very expensive, about $500,000. What does the writer argue has to happen? _____

4. Doctors had to operate on Mr. Baugh so they could find the nerves where his arms once were. What does the writer argue? _____

5. In the future, scientists think people could control the prosthetics by a device they wear on their head. What does the writer argue is needed? _____

◉ Reading 2

A. Preview the text. Then read it on your own.

Helping the Deaf to Feel and See Sound

Stop and Think

What other things can we do to help deaf people?

As a teacher, I wanted to make a difference in my students' lives, so I asked a friend of a friend to visit my classroom. This woman was deaf. She had been unable to **hear** her whole life. She used sign language to communicate. My friend who understands sign language translated for her. I thought my students would benefit from hearing her story. The woman came into the classroom and sat down on one of the old classroom chairs. She said she knew the chair was squeaky even though she couldn't hear. She said she could tell from the way the chair moved. She also said that once when she was downtown in the city, a bus went by. She had her back to the street so she didn't see it, but she felt the ground **shake**. She can't hear sounds, but she feels them.

Now there are **devices** that allow deaf people to feel and see sounds. Imagine this: A person finishes giving a presentation and the room fills with clapping. Everyone claps, including the deaf people. They feel the sound. A new device that they wear on their wrists vibrates, or shakes, when there are loud sounds. Little lights on it also flash. Even without hearing, the person is **able to** feel connected to the group, to be a part of what is happening. This small device could also save their lives. A bus honks its horn or a fire alarm goes off. The deaf person feels it and sees the lights flashing. And while many devices to help deaf people are **expensive**, this one isn't. It's about $137. Another device allows deaf people to see sound. Developers put very small microphones, devices for picking up sound, on a pair of glasses. When a loud or dangerous sound is close, small lights in the glasses flash. A bus comes too close and the lights flash.

The person steps back. A life is saved.

Many of these devices are just ideas. As a result, we need businesses to give their money and time to develop them. The problem is that many businesses don't think they will earn enough money from them. Although there are many people who could benefit (about 360 million people in the world are deaf), many cannot **afford** the devices available now. However, this might be changing. As the world creates more **advanced** technology, deaf people will be able to benefit. For example, texting and communicating by email have already made it easier for deaf people to talk to others. Other developments are helping too. One business created a product for people who listen to loud music on their earphones. The device vibrates to let them know if the music is too loud. The business saw that this idea could help deaf people too. If more people learn about the lives of deaf people, then they will develop devices to help them. In addition, as technology becomes less expensive, more people can create, share, and buy new products. There is an opportunity to make a real difference in deaf people's lives.

Deaf people use sign language to communicate. An interpreter tells hearing people what the deaf person says.

Grammar in the Readings

Notice *could, should,* and *will have to* to discuss possibility and argue a point in the readings.

Could, should, and *will* are used to show possibility or argument. Writers use *could* + verb to show that something is possible in the future.

*New prosthetics **could make** life easier.*

Writers use *should* + verb to make an argument.

*Scientists **should concentrate** on creating safe prosthetics.*

Writers use *will have to* + verb to make a very strong argument and show there is no other possibility.

*Because of this, scientists **will have to make** changes.*

GO ONLINE
for grammar practice

Check Your Understanding

B. Complete each sentence with a word or phrase from the box. One word or phrase will not be used.

afford	deaf person	device	flash
ground	pick up	teacher	~~vibrate~~

1. The word _____vibrate_____ has the same meaning as *shake*.

2. The writer is a(n) _____ .

3. The deaf woman heard a bus go by because she felt the _____ shake.

4. A new device helps deaf people. It can vibrate and _____ .

5. A microphone is a small _____ . It is used to _____ sounds.

6. One big problem with many of these devices is that deaf people can't

_____ them.

Recycle

the Vocabulary Strategy

Vocabulary Strategy: Use Negative Prefixes

C. Circle the correct word to complete each sentence about the text on pages 88–89.

1. Using a device that vibrates is one way to help deaf people feel
   (connected) *disconnected* to society.

2. The writer thinks it is *safe   unsafe* to not be able to hear in a busy city.

3. The writer thinks many of the devices are *helpful   unhelpful*.

4. The writer lists the cost of a small device that is *expensive   inexpensive*.

Recycle

the Reading Strategy

Reading Strategy: Recognize Argument

D. Match each question to the writer's argument. Reread the text on pages 88–89 if needed.

Question

1. __b__ What does the writer argue is possible with the vibrating, flashing device people wear on their wrists?

2. _____ Many of the devices are just ideas. What does the writer argue?

3. _____ What does the writer argue will be the result if more people learn about deaf people?

4. _____ The writer says that technology is becoming more advanced and less expensive. What does she argue is the result?

Argument

a. People will create devices to help them.

b. ~~It will save people's lives.~~

c. New devices can make a difference in deaf people's lives.

d. Businesses need to give time and money to develop these devices.

● Make Connections: Text to Text

A. Both writers use arguments. Answer the questions to analyze the arguments.

1. Which text do you think has a stronger argument? For instance, do you think it's more important to give money to developing prosthetics or devices for the deaf?

_____

_____

2. For the argument you chose in question 1, what information made the argument strong? List details from the reading that changed your thinking.

_____

_____

3. What information do you think the writer of the text with the weaker argument should have included? For instance, what information would make that argument stronger?

_____

_____

B. Both writers use stories about people. Complete the web to describe the person in each text.

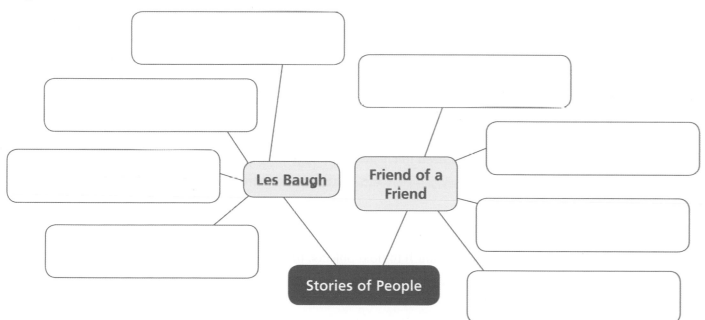

C. Compare your web from Activity B with a partner. Discuss the effect of these stories. Why did the writer include each person's story in the text? How do the stories make you feel?

Summarizing and Retelling

A. Complete the sentences with the words from the box. Some of the words have to be changed to fit the sentences. For example, *device* has to be changed to *devices*. Then read the paragraphs to a partner to summarize.

Adjectives	Nouns	Verbs
able	device	afford
advanced	hope	hear
expensive		operate
permanent		shake

1.   There is _____ for people who have lost limbs. Scientists are working on _____ prosthetics to help them. Because they are so advanced, they are also _____ . In addition, doctors now have to _____ on people to attach them. However, we can change this if we give the time and money needed. In the future, people may be _____ to walk again or hold babies. Losing a limb does not have to be _____ .

2.   There are _____ to help people who can't _____ . One device _____ when a loud sound is near. This device is not expensive. And yet a problem is that many deaf people cannot _____ the devices. We need to create technology to help them and make the devices less expensive.

B. Both writers contrast ideas. Match the sentence parts to show the contrasts.

1. He has used his mouth to hold objects, to cook, to do all the other things we use our hands for; _____

2. The devices won't be as advanced, _____

3. And while many devices to help deaf people are expensive, _____

4. Although many people could benefit (about 360 million people in the world are deaf), _____

a. but they will cost less.

b. however, medical developments are changing this.

c. many cannot afford the devices available now.

d. this one isn't.

Word Partners

be able to

better able to

feel able to

perfectly able to

seem able to

_____

GO ONLINE
to practice
word partners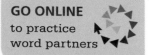

● **Make Connections:** Text to World

A. When do writers use arguments? Share your ideas with a partner.

1. _____

2. _____

3. _____

4. _____

5. _____

B. Use ideas from the text and your own ideas to complete the web. Look at the Oxford 2000 keywords on page 133 and find five words to help you.

Deaf people can
communicate by texting.

_____
_____

_____
_____

How can technology help people who are disabled?

_____
_____

_____
_____

_____
_____

C. Think about texts with arguments. What makes the argument strong?

1. The writer talks about _____

2. The writer _____

3. The writer _____

Chant

GO ONLINE
for the
Chapter 6
Vocabulary &
Grammar Chant

Look at the word bank for Unit 2. Check (✓) the words you know.
Circle the words you want to learn better.

OXFORD 2000 🔑			
Adjectives	**Nouns**		**Verbs**
able (to)	competition	opportunity	afford
advanced	culture	project	belong
available	device	society	earn
easy	difference	tradition	fit (in)
expensive	fashion	value	follow
lonely	hope		hear
permanent	human		increase
	Internet		operate
	message		shake
	nature		

PRACTICE WITH THE OXFORD 2000 🔑

A. Use the words in the chart. Match adjectives with nouns.

1. _____easy project_____   2. _____

3. _____   4. _____

5. _____

B. Use the words in the chart. Match verbs with nouns.

1. _____fit in society_____   2. _____

3. _____   4. _____

5. _____

C. Use the words in the chart. Match verbs with adjective noun partners.

1. _afford expensive fashion_   2. _____

3. _____   4. _____

5. _____

UNIT **3** Problems and Solutions

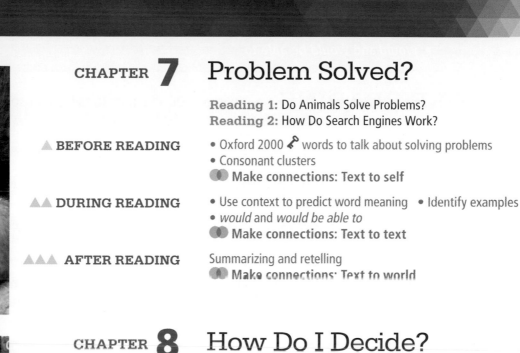

UNIT WRAP UP Extend Your Skills

- Consonant clusters
- Use context to predict word meaning
- Identify examples
- *would* and *would be able to*

▲ BEFORE READING ▶ Oxford 2000 ✎ words to talk about solving problems

Learn Vocabulary

A. Read the definitions and look at the picture. Complete the paragraph with the bold words from the box.

To **ignore** is to know about something but not use or do anything about it.

To **list** is to write or say many things one after another.

To **refer to** something is to talk about or write about it.

A **search engine** is a computer program that looks for information on the Internet.

Many people search for answers to questions on the Internet. A popular _____ is

Google. In fact, Google is also used as a verb. To "Google" something is to search for it. Search engines

like Google _____ web pages that answer your question. These are called the *results.*

Results _____ all the web pages that the search engine found. Most often this

information is helpful. However, you may have to _____ some results because the

information does not answer your question. While search engines are helpful, you still need to review the

results and figure out what is important.

B. Read the definitions and look at the pictures. Complete the paragraph with the bold words from the box.

Something that is **huge** is very big.

A human or animal that is **intelligent** is able to think, understand, and learn quickly.

A **solution** is an answer to a question or problem.

A **tool** is something you use to do a task.

A problem is a question you have. When you **solve problems**, you find answers.

To **survive** is to continue to live.

Elephants are _____ animals. They spend 80 percent of their day eating. They need hundreds of pounds of fruit to _____. In an experiment, researchers wanted to show that elephants can _____. An elephant could not get fruit from a tree. It was too high. The elephant pushed a block over to the tree. Then it stood on the block and got the fruit. The elephant showed it was _____. It found a(n) _____ to its problem. It used a block as a(n) _____ to stand on.

C. Describe what the chimpanzee in the picture is doing. Use four bold words from the boxes in Activities A and B. Compare your description with a partner.

Oxford 2000 🔑

Use the Oxford 2000 list on page 133 to find more words to describe the pictures on these pages. Share your words with a partner.

GO ONLINE for more practice

_____

_____

Preview the Text

D. Look at the picture and text on page 100. Answer the questions.

1. What does the picture show? _____

_____

2. Why is the picture important to the text? _____

_____

3. The first sentence of the text is "What do humans do that shows we are intelligent?"

Answer the question. _____

_____

E. Circle the best answer.

1. Why do you think the writer wrote this text?

   a. He wants to show that animals are intelligent.

   b. He wants to explain why elephants are the most intelligent animals.

   c. He wants to argue that some animals are not intelligent.

2. What do you think the writer will use to support the text?

   a. stories from his life

   b. research results and experiments

   c. jokes

Sounds of English

Spelling Connection

🔊 A. Listen to the word *think*. The consonants *nk* at the end of the word form a cluster. A consonant cluster can be at the beginning, middle, or end of a word. Some consonants form one sound, like the *th* at the beginning of *think*. However, in consonant clusters, you can hear the separate sounds of the consonants. Listen to these words. Notice the sounds in the consonant clusters. They are in the same syllable.

permane**nt**   **tr**end   object   experime**nt**   **pr**oje**ct**

Note that when the consonant *r* has a vowel before it, the vowel is *r*-controlled. It has the sound of the *r*. The *r* is not part of a consonant cluster.

🔊 B. Listen to the words. Circle the words that have a consonant cluster. Underline the words that have an *r*-controlled vowel.

intelligent   problem   search   survive

C. These words are in the text on page 100. Underline each consonant cluster.

brain   chimpanzees   creative   protect   snake   step stool

⬤ Make Connections: Text to Self

A. Check the statements you agree with. Then discuss your ideas with a partner. Share examples to support your opinion.

1. _____ Solving problems shows creativity.

2. _____ Animals are interesting.

3. _____ Animals solve problems in interesting ways.

4. _____ Animals use tools effectively.

B. How do animals solve problems? List some ways.

1. They use tools. _____

2. _____

3. _____

4. _____

5. _____

C. List three animals that you think can solve problems and the types of problems they solve.

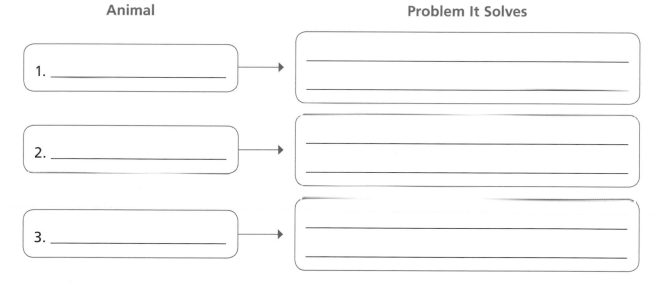

Animal   Problem It Solves

1. _____

2. _____

3. _____

◉ **Reading 1**

A. Read the text on your own. Focus on meaning. Slow down and reread phrases and sentences if you don't understand.

Do Animals Solve Problems?

Some dolphins put sponges on their snouts to protect them as they look for food on the sea floor.

Stop and Think

Do you agree? Does using tools show problem solving?

What do humans do that shows we are **intelligent**? One thing we do is **solve problems**. When there is a problem, it is human nature to look for a **solution**. We solve problems every day at school, work, and home. What about animals? Can they solve problems? One way scientists identify intelligence in animals is by seeing if they use **tools**. Why is this a sign of intelligence? Using tools shows creative thinking. Animals use tools for basic problem solving so they can **survive**. For instance, chimpanzees take the leaves off sticks and then use the sticks to dig in the dirt and find bugs to eat. Some dolphins use sponges to cover their snouts as they look for food on the ocean floor. This shows problem solving. A dolphin can hurt its snout while looking for food, so it covers it to protect it. A mother elephant at a zoo had a problem. Her baby was small and couldn't get the mother's milk. The mother moved a block so the baby could stand on it and get the milk. This solved the problem. Scientists often use these animals in experiments because these animals show other signs of intelligence: Chimps have learned sign language, and dolphins have an advanced way of communicating using sounds. Elephants communicate with one another, too, and often work together in teams to protect each other from lions and other dangerous animals.

Other animals also show some creative problem solving. For example, crows are very good at using tools. In one experiment, a crow used a piece of wire to get food from the bottom of a long tube. Squirrels also show some intelligent thinking. Some squirrels rub the skins of rattlesnakes on their bodies. Then animals that eat squirrels don't smell them. Instead, they smell the rattlesnake skin.

Using tools can show creative thinking. However, using tools isn't the only way to see if animals can solve problems. Cephalopods, which are squids, octopuses, and other creatures without backbones, have **huge** brains. They show advanced thinking. In one experiment, scientists wanted to see if an octopus would be able to take a lid off a jar. They put food in the jar and screwed on the lid. The octopus used its arms to unscrew the lid. First, though, it turned the lid the wrong way. Then it figured out which way to unscrew it. Problems are a part of life for any living thing, and animals will do what they need to survive. Whether it's using tools or their own bodies, they solve problems. Some are quite good at it.

B. Now read the text again. This time focus on speed. You understand the ideas. You can read faster. You don't need to say each word.

Check Your Understanding

C. Complete the outline with ideas from the text on page 100.

I. Animals are intelligent because they _____.

  A. They use _____, which shows creativity.

    1. Examples of intelligent animals using tools

      a. Chimpanzees _____.

      b. Dolphins _____.

      c. An elephant mother _____.

    2. Examples of other animals using tools

      a. _____ use wire to get food from a long tube.

      b. Squirrels _____.

  B. Animals use their bodies to solve problems.

    1. In one experiment, _____.

Vocabulary Strategy

Use Context to Predict Word Meaning

Many times you can understand a word's meaning by looking at how it's used in a sentence. The sentence and other sentences around a word are called the *context*. Use the context to help you understand a word's meaning.

1. Read the sentence the word is in.
2. Figure out the part of speech. Is the word a *noun*, *adjective*, *verb*, or *adverb* in this context? Look for suffixes and verb endings to help you.
3. Try to think of a word or phrase that means the same thing.
4. Reread the sentence and replace the word with another word or phrase. Does the sentence have the same meaning?

GO ONLINE
for more practice

D. Find each word in the text on page 100. Read the context and then match each word to its part of speech and meaning.

1. __c__ sign

2. _____ basic

3. _____ protect

4. _____ screw

5. _____ hurt

a. *(v.)* to turn something to attach it to another thing

b. *(v.)* to feel pain

c. *(n.)* ~~something that tells you something is true~~

d. *(adj.)* simple, including what is necessary

e. *(v.)* to keep something safe

Reading Strategy

Identify Examples

Writers give examples to support their ideas. An example shows the reader what the writer is talking about.

1. Many times, examples begin with signal words like *for example* or *for instance*. Often the example comes after the statement it supports.

   Animals use tools for basic problem solving so they can survive. **For instance**, *chimpanzees take the leaves off sticks and then use the sticks to dig in the dirt and find bugs to eat.*

2. Other times the example is not introduced with signal words. However, you can identify the example because it supports the statement before it. Examples may:

   - use proper nouns or name specific things.

     And some **dolphins** *use* **sponges** *to cover their snouts as they look for food on the sea floor.*

   - talk about a specific event, time, or place.

     In **one experiment**, *a crow used a piece of wire to get food from the bottom of a long tube.*

Use these tips to look for examples. Then ask yourself what the example supports. This can help you understand the writer's ideas.

GO ONLINE
for more
practice

E. Read each group of sentences. Is the sentence an example or the idea the example supports? Label the example *E* and the idea *I*. Underline words to help you identify the example.

1. __I__ Animals use tools for basic problem solving so they can survive.

   __E__ For instance, chimpanzees take the leaves off sticks and then use the sticks to dig in the dirt and find bugs to eat.

2. _____ This shows problem solving.

   _____ A dolphin can hurt its snout while looking for food, so it covers it to protect it.

3. _____ Scientists often use these animals in experiments because these animals show other signs of intelligence.

   _____ Chimps have learned sign language, and dolphins have an advanced way of communicating using sounds.

4. _____ Other animals also show some creative problem solving.

   _____ For example, crows are very good at using tools.

5. _____ Cephalopods, which are squids, octopuses, and other creatures without backbones, have huge brains. They show advanced thinking.

   _____ In one experiment, scientists wanted to see if an octopus would be able to take a lid off a jar . . . The octopus used its arms to unscrew the lid.

Reading 2

A. Preview the text. Then read it to yourself. Focus on the meaning.

How Do Search Engines Work?

How do you search for information on the Internet? Many people use the popular website Google, but there are many other **search engines** available. Try it now. Think of a problem you want to **solve** or information you want to know. What do you type to get your information? Children and younger people often type a complete question. For example, "What should I do if I'm swimming and a shark is near?" Adults often have more experience using technology and will type in only the most important words: "swimming with sharks safety." Both ways will get results. But using the key words usually gets results faster. If you did type in a question, the search engines often **ignore** the punctuation and words that aren't nouns or verbs. Search engines use programs called web crawlers to look at web pages. The programs search for the key words, like "kinds of sharks," and then send web pages back to the search engine. The program works well. Even if you misspell a word like "sharks" as "shakrs," it can predict the word.

Search engines use the programs to make indexes. An index is a copy of web pages and the Internet addresses of them. Search engines have **huge** indexes. When a program visits a web page, it adds it to the index. Then it follows links on those pages to other web pages and adds these to the index. So when you type in a question or key words, the search engine looks through this huge index. This is why it's important to be very detailed in your web searches. For example, if you want to know what kinds of sharks you might see in the Atlantic Ocean near Key West, Florida, your search should say, "sharks in the Atlantic Ocean near Key West" and not "kinds of sharks." However, even this detailed search shows more than 250,000 results. How do you know which articles to read? The search engine **lists** the sites that have the most links to them first. This means that other web pages **refer to** them. Because other sites refer to them, these links may be a good place to start.

Other things also affect the order the sites are listed in. If someone does not update the information on the web site, then it may be lower in the results. Punctuation can also affect the results. For instance, using a dash before a word tells the search engine to ignore it. This is helpful for searches with words that have multiple meaning words. What would happen if you searched for "beetle"? You might get results describing the big black bug. But you could also get results showing the popular type of car also called a "Beetle." By placing a dash before the word—"-car"—you tell the search engine to ignore the word *car*. Now, it's possible to learn anything you want on the Internet. It helps to know how best to search for it.

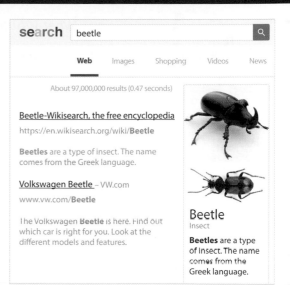

A search engine orders the links to web pages in a list. These are the results of a web search. You can click on a link to go to each web page.

Stop and Think

How do you search for information on the Internet?

B. Read the text again. Now focus on speed. You can read faster now that you understand the ideas.

Grammar in the Readings

Notice *would* and *would be able to* in the readings.

Writers use *would* and *would be able* to when they explain a future result. *Would* explains that the idea hasn't happened yet.

> What **would** <u>happen</u> if you searched for "beetle"?

Use *would be able to* + verb to talk about a future ability that has not happened yet.

> In one experiment, scientists wanted to see if an octopus **would be able to** <u>take</u> a lid off a jar.

GO ONLINE
for grammar practice

Check Your Understanding

C. Write a short answer to each question.

1. What are key words? _____

2. What are web crawlers? _____

3. What's an index? _____

4. What sites does a web search list first? _____

5. How can you make a search engine ignore a word? _____

Recycle

the Vocabulary Strategy

Vocabulary Strategy: Use Context to Predict Word Meaning

D. Find each word below in the text on page 103. Read the context and then match each word to its meaning.

1. __c__ popular
2. _____ program
3. _____ detailed
4. _____ update
5. _____ lower

a. *(adj.)* giving a lot of information

b. *(adj.)* that is under something or at the bottom of something

c. ~~*(adj.)* liked or used by a lot of people~~

d. *(n.)* a set of instructions that you give a computer

e. *(v.)* to add new information to something

Recycle

the Reading Strategy

Reading Strategy: Identify Examples

E. Read the examples. Write a sentence or phrase from the text on page 103 that the example supports.

1. For example, "What should I do if I'm swimming and a shark is near?" _____

_____

2. "swimming with sharks safety" _____

_____

3. Even if you misspell a word like "sharks" as "shakrs," it can predict the word. _____

_____

4. For example, if you want to know what kinds of sharks you might see in the Atlantic Ocean near Key West, Florida, your search should say, "sharks in the Atlantic Ocean near Key West" and not "kinds of sharks." _____

_____

● Make Connections: Text to Text

A. Both texts talk about problems and solutions. For each problem listed, write the solution. Tell how the animal solves the problem in Reading 1 and how the web program or person solves the problem in Reading 2.

Problems	Solutions
1. Chimpanzees need to get their favorite food that lives underground.	1. _____
2. A mother elephant's baby can't reach her milk.	2. _____
3. A crow can't get its food at the bottom of a tube.	3. _____
4. A child writes a whole question into a search engine, including punctuation.	4. _____
5. Someone misspells a word in a web search.	5. _____
6. The search engine finds thousands of web page results.	6. _____

B. Both writers use *this* to refer back to ideas in the text. Match the word *this* in each sentence to the idea it refers to.

1. _____ **This** shows problem solving.

2. _____ **This** is why it's important to be very detailed in your web searches.

3. _____ **This** means that other web pages refer to them.

4. _____ **This** is helpful for searches with words that have multiple meanings.

   a. The mother moved a block so the baby could stand on it and reach the milk.

   b. Using a dash before a word tells the search engine to ignore it.

   c. When you type in a question or key words, the search engine looks through this huge index.

   d. The search engine lists the sites that have the most links to them first.

Summarizing and Retelling

A. Complete the sentences with the words from the box. Some of the words have to be changed to fit the sentences. For example, *problem* has to be changed to *problems*. Then read the paragraphs to a partner to summarize.

Adjectives	Nouns	Verbs
huge	problem	ignore
intelligent	search engine	list
	solution	refer
	tool	survive

1. The first text discusses if animals solve _____ . The writer gives examples of animals that use _____ . This shows that they are _____ . The writer shows that many animals solve problems to _____ .

2. The second text discusses how _____ work. The writer tells about programs that create _____ indexes. These indexes _____ to all the web pages that have the key words from the search. The program usually _____ punctuation. It _____ the results, but there can still be thousands of results. How can you get the results you want? One _____ is to use punctuation to make the program ignore words.

Word Partners

come up with a solution

look for a solution

perfect solution

work toward a solution

GO ONLINE to practice word partners

B. Answer the questions.

1. The writer discusses examples of animals solving problems. What example do you think is the strongest? _____

2. The writer gives examples for how search engines work. Which example do you think is the most helpful? _____

● Make Connections: Text to World

A. Think about the two texts. Complete the web.

_____

_____

Why do writers use examples?

_____

_____

B. Check the types of texts where examples are most helpful. For each type that you check, list an example you find in that type of text.

1. ___✓___ to explain how to do something _There are examples of search results in_
texts on how to use search engines.

2. _____ to explain why something happens _____

_____

3. _____ to talk about an animal's behavior and actions _____

_____

4. _____ to describe an event _____

_____

5. _____ to tell about a famous person _____

_____

C. Complete the web. Write an idea for a text in the center circle. Then list examples you would include in the outer circles. Look at the Oxford 2000 keywords on page 133 and find five words to help you.

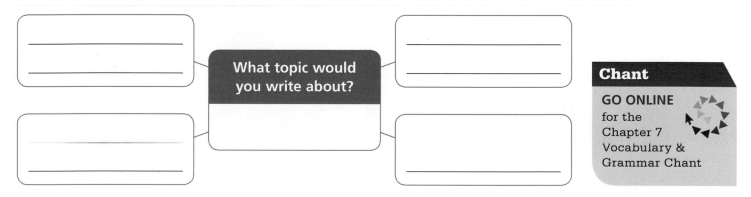

_____

_____

What topic would you write about?

_____

_____

Chant

GO ONLINE
for the
Chapter 7
Vocabulary &
Grammar Chant

CHAPTER 8 How Do I Decide?

- Recognize /y/
- Words with multiple meanings
- Compare and contrast
- Past perfect with *so* and *because*

▲ BEFORE READING ▸ Oxford 2000 ✎ words to talk about making decisions

Learn Vocabulary

A. Match each picture to the correct description.

_____ My pay **depends on** the number of computers I sell.

_____ I found the **perfect** laptop. It's small and fits into my bag.

_____ My **behavior** changes when I am with my friends. I talk louder and laugh a lot.

__1__ I don't know Matt well, but he **seems like** a nice person.

1.

2.

3.
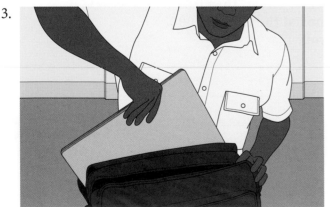

4.

B. Read the definitions and look at the picture. Complete the paragraph with the bold words and phrase from the box.

choices: the things you can choose from

confuse: to mix someone's ideas so that he or she cannot think clearly or understand

make a decision: to choose something after thinking about it

I don't like shopping at big stores. When there are so many _____, I don't know what to buy. It's difficult to _____. Sometimes I leave the store without buying anything! Too many choices _____ me. It's easier to shop at smaller stores. There aren't as many choices, and it's easier for me to make decisions.

Oxford 2000 🔑

Use the Oxford 2000 list on page 133 to find more words to describe the pictures on these pages. Share your words with a partner.

C. When something is *likely*, it will probably happen. When you feel *certain*, you are sure about it. It will happen. Circle the answer to describe you.

1. I am *certain* *likely* *not likely* to go on vacation this year.

2. I am *certain* *likely* *not likely* to live in another country in my life.

3. I am *certain* *likely* *not likely* to buy something expensive this year.

4. I am *certain* *likely* *not likely* to talk to my friend tonight.

5. I am *certain* *likely* *not likely* to have a test this week.

GO ONLINE for more practice

Preview the Text

D. Look at the pictures and text on page 112. Answer the questions.

1. What does the top photo show? _____

_____

2. What does the bottom photo show? _____

_____

3. Look at the pictures and title of the text. Write an idea for another photo the writer

   could use. _____

_____

E. Answer the questions.

1. Which word in the sentences that follow has the same meaning as *choices*? *In some countries, there are more than 200 types of cereal on the shelf. How can anyone make a decision with that many options?* _____

2. Read the title and predict the answer in the text. _____

3. Which word in the sentence that follows has the same meaning as *customers*? *This is because they think consumers will be more likely to buy something if they have options.*

   _____

4. Which word in the sentence that follows has the same meaning as *happiness*? *So while it seems like more choices would lead to greater satisfaction, this is not the case.*

   _____

Sounds of English

Spelling Connection

🔊 A. Listen to the word *vocabulary*. Do you hear the /y/ sound after the /b/? The letter *y* is not there, but the /y/ sound is added between the consonant *b* and the schwa sound that follows.

Listen for the added /y/ sound in the words below. Draw an arrow to show where it is added.

   beautiful   computer   figure   opinion   usual

🔊 B. Listen to the words. Circle the words that have an added /y/ sound. Draw an arrow to show where it is added.

   behavior   certain   choices   confuse   likely

C. These words are in the text on page 112. Circle the word with an added /y/ sound. Draw an arrow to show where it is.

   business   customer   similarly   university

⬤ Make Connections: Text to Self

A. Think about yourself. Check the statements that describe you.

1. _____ I like to have many choices when I am buying something.

2. _____ I make decisions quickly.

3. _____ In most cases, I am happy with the decisions I make.

4. _____ If I don't have choices, I can't get the perfect product.

5. _____ I do a lot of research before I buy a product.

B. For some products, like cereal, there are many choices. List other products that have many choices available. Look at the Oxford 2000 keywords on page 133 and find words to help you.

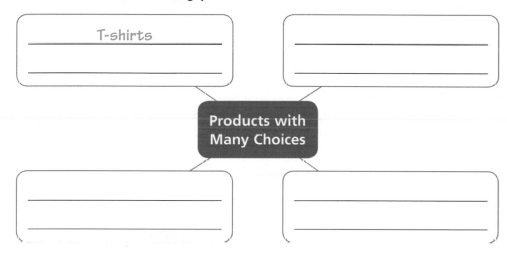

T-shirts

Products with Many Choices

C. For some products, there aren't that many choices. What products do you wish stores had more choices for?

1. _____

2. _____

3. _____

D. Answer the questions. Then discuss your answers with a partner. Provide examples to support your opinions.

1. Do businesses sell more products when they provide more choices to customers?

_____

2. Are people more likely to buy a product if there are more choices? Why or why not?

_____

3. Does having more choices for products make people happier? Why or why not?

_____

◉ Reading 1

A. Some words are often part of a phrase. We call them *fixed phrases*. Fixed phrases like *in fact*, *the fact is*, and *this is not the case* connect ideas in sentences. Listen to how the fixed phrases are read.

Are More Choices Better?

Supermarket aisles are filled with products. It's hard to make decisions with so many choices.

Stop and Think

Why is making decisions confusing?

Which jar of jam would you buy?

You run into the store to buy a box of cereal. You want something healthy that also tastes good. You know what you like, but ten minutes go by and you are still standing in the aisle. Why? In some countries, there are more than 200 types of cereal on the shelf. How can anyone **make a decision** with that many options? You have more **choices**, but you spend more time making a decision. Are more choices always better?

Yes. If you don't have a choice, you have to buy that one product. Then the company that makes that product gets all the business. There's no competition. In addition, there's no way to know if you are getting the best product. This is what some people think. They want choices because they like to research options. They want to find the **perfect** product. Today that seems possible. There is more product information available than at any time in history. You can read product reviews of everything online. Therefore, having choices means you'll find the best product for you. With more than 200 kinds of cereal, you can certainly find the perfect one, right?

Likewise, many businesses think more options are better. If they don't provide choices, they won't sell products. This is because they think consumers will be more **likely** to buy something if they have options. However, studies show this isn't true. When customers had the choice of six

different jams, 30 percent bought a jar. In contrast, when there were 24 different jams to choose from, only 3 percent of customers bought one! People didn't buy the jam because they felt less **certain** of what they liked. In fact, they had not made a decision because too many choices **confused** them.

So, while it **seems like** more choices would lead to greater satisfaction, this is not the case. On the contrary, more choices bring less satisfaction. The more options you have, the harder it is to decide. And once you've finally made your decision, the less certain you are about your choice. This is true for small decisions like what cereal or jam to buy but also big decisions like what university to go to. If you have a lot of choices, the questions remain: Did you choose the right thing? Did you make the best decision? These questions make people unhappy. They start to feel that maybe another choice would have been better. They begin to wish they had tried something different. Now researchers are telling people to ask, "Was my choice good enough?" The fact is there are going to be advantages and disadvantages to every decision. Understanding this can help people feel better about their choices. Similarly, businesses can also benefit from understanding the difficulty people have with making decisions. Maybe providing a few good options instead of many is the best solution.

B. Read the text on your own. What ideas do the fixed phrases connect in the text?

Check Your Understanding

C. Circle the correct answer.

1. What does *the company* probably refer to?

   (a.) a business   b. customers

2. People are _____ likely to buy something if there are more choices.

   a. less   b. more

3. What does it mean to choose something that is *good enough*?

   a. There is a perfect choice for you.   b. No choice is perfect.

4. Based on the text, which strategy do you recommend to businesses?

   a. Provide many colors and types of your product.

   b. Show fewer than ten different colors or types of your product.

Vocabulary Strategy

Words with Multiple Meanings

Some words can be used as different parts of speech. The meaning is similar. Recognizing words with multiple meanings will help you not confuse them when you read.

noun	verb
However, **studies** show this isn't true.	He **studies** biology at the university.
study: (n.) a piece of research done to learn	study: (v.) to spend time learning about something

Some word forms are the same, but the meanings are not.

adjective	adjective
The more options you have, the **harder** it is to decide.	The ground is **harder** than the grass.
hard: (adj.) difficult to do or understand	hard: (adj.) not soft

GO ONLINE
for more
practice

D. Read each sentence and circle the meaning of the underlined word.

1. There is more product information available today than at any <u>time</u> in history.

   a. a certain point in the day or night that you say in hours and minutes

   (b.) a period in the past; a part of history

2. So while it seems like more choices would <u>lead</u> to satisfaction, this is not the case.

   a. to make something happen

   b. to take a person or animal somewhere by going with them or in front of them

3. You can read product <u>reviews</u> of almost anything online.

   a. a piece of writing that says what someone thinks

   b. to study something to make sure you remember or understand it

Compare and Contrast

Writers often compare and contrast ideas. When they compare ideas, they tell what is the same or similar. When they contrast ideas, they concentrate on the differences. Learn signal words and phrases to help you know when an author is comparing and contrasting information.

These signal words and phrases are often used for comparing and contrasting.

Compare	Contrast	
in the same manner	*but*	*while*
in like manner	*however*	*yet*
likewise	*in contrast*	
similar / similarly	*on the contrary*	

GO ONLINE
for more
practice

E. Read the sentences. Underline the signal word or phrase. Write *Contrast* or *Compare*. Then discuss with a partner the difference or similarity the sentences describe.

1. ___Contrast___ So while it seems like more choices would lead to greater satisfaction, this is not the case. <u>On the contrary</u>, more choices bring less satisfaction.

2. _____ With more than 200 kinds of cereal, you can certainly find the perfect one, right? Likewise, many businesses think more options are better.

3. _____ This is because they think consumers will be more likely to buy something if they have options. However, studies show this isn't true.

4. _____ So while it seems like more choices would lead to greater satisfaction, this is not the case.

◉ Reading 2

A. Phrases used to compare and contrast are also fixed phrases. Read the text. Focus on the fixed phrases and how they connect ideas.

Do Your Decisions Make You Happy?

Stop and Think

Which of the two groups described in the reading do you fit in?

Think of the last big purchase you made. Maybe it was clothing or a new phone or computer. How long did it take you to **make the decision**? Did you research other **choices**? How many? How you make decisions may be connected to your happiness. Researchers divide people into two groups. The people in the first group research every option. They look at every choice because they don't want to miss the **perfect** one. They read reviews on the Internet, talk to people, and weigh all their options before they make their decision. The people in the second group also want to make a good decision; however, they want to do it quickly. They want to make a choice that is good enough but that does not take too much time. In contrast to the first group, they want to make their decision and move on. Do you know which group you belong in? Your **behavior** may **depend on** the purchase you are making. For example, maybe you make decisions quickly when you are at the grocery store but take more time when buying a more expensive item like a TV. Even if this is the case, most people fall into one of the two groups most of the time.

Researchers studied people from each group. They found that people in one group are no more **likely** to make bad decisions than the other. Yet they did find a difference in happiness between the two groups. Despite the fact that those in the first group who examine every option got better jobs, they were less satisfied. They were offered jobs that paid 20 percent more than the other group of fast decision makers. Yet later they didn't feel good about themselves or their jobs. The researchers of the study said that these people made good decisions but didn't like that they had to choose one job instead of another. After they had made their decision, they spent a lot of time thinking about the other choices. They weren't **certain** they had made the best choice, so they felt less happy. The researchers reported that the second group was happier more often. Perhaps this is because they spent less time worrying about their decision. They made their choice and stopped thinking about it. Interestingly, researchers found that as people get older, they are more likely to be in the second group. With time, people see there is often no perfect solution, and in the same manner, they learn to feel OK with their choice.

Grammar in the Readings

Notice past perfect with *so* and *because* in the readings.

The past perfect tense shows that one action was completed before a second action. Writers often use the past perfect tense with *so* and *because* to explain a reason.

> They weren't certain they <u>had made</u> the best choice, **so** they felt less happy.
> They <u>had not made</u> a decision **because** too many choices confused them.

GO ONLINE
for grammar practice

Check Your Understanding

B. Write *T* (true) or *F* (false). Rewrite false statements to be true.

1. __F__ You always belong in one of the two groups because your behavior is the same for every purchase.

You often belong in one of the two groups, but your behavior may depend on the purchase.

2. _____ In contrast to people in the first group, those in the second group do a lot of research.

_____

3. _____ People who make fast decisions are more likely to make bad decisions.

_____

4. _____ People in the two groups have differences in how happy they are with their choices.

_____

Vocabulary Strategy: Words with Multiple Meanings

C. Read the first sentence. Circle the sentence that uses the same meaning of the underlined word.

1. Think of the last big <u>purchase</u> you made.

   a. He purchased a new car.   b. She made a few large purchases last month.

2. How <u>long</u> did it take you to make the decision?

   a. How long is the Amazon River?   b. How long was your vacation?

3. Despite the fact that those in the first group who <u>examine</u> every option got better jobs, they were less satisfied.

   a. You will be examined on everything you have learned in this chapter.

   b. We asked someone to examine our house before we bought it.

4. They read reviews on the Internet, talk to people, and <u>weigh</u> all their options before they make their decision.

   a. She weighed the advantages and disadvantages of both jobs before choosing one.

   b. She weighed the box before she sent it.

Reading Strategy: Compare and Contrast

D. Read the sentences. Underline the signal word or phrase. Write *Contrast* or *Compare*. Then discuss with a partner the difference or similarity the sentences describe.

1. ___Contrast___ The people in the second group also want to make a good decision; however, they want to do it quickly.

2. _____ They found that people in one group are no more likely to make bad decisions than the other. Yet they did find a difference in happiness between the two groups.

3. _____ They were offered jobs that paid 20 percent more than the other group of fast decision makers. Yet later they didn't feel good about themselves or their jobs.

4. _____ The researchers of the study said that these people made good decisions but didn't like that they had to choose one job instead of another.

5. _____ With time, people see there is often no perfect solution, and in the same manner, they learn to feel OK with their choice.

● Make Connections: Text to Text

A. Both texts compare and contrast ideas. Think about the main ideas in each text. Summarize what is being compared and contrasted.

"Are More Choices Better?"	"Do Your Decisions Make You Happy?"

B. Both texts show results from studies. Check the conclusions that are supported by the text. Then write *1* for Reading 1, *2* for Reading 2, or *B* for both.

1. _____ Businesses should provide a small number of product options.

2. _____ People should make a decision and not keep thinking about it.

3. _____ People should not look at every option possible.

4. _____ People should choose something that is good enough.

5. _____ People should research only a small number of products to choose from.

C. Both writers use *more* or *less* to describe how likely or certain something is. Complete each sentence with a phrase from the box.

less likely	more likely	less certain	more certain

1. People are _____ of what to buy when there are not too many options.

2. People are _____ to be unhappy with their product if they researched many options.

3. People who research many options are _____ they made the right choice.

4. People who see a lot of choices are _____ to buy something.

Summarizing and Retelling

A. Complete the sentences with the words from the box. Some of the words have to be changed to fit the sentences. For example, *choice* has to be changed to *choices*. Then read the paragraphs to a partner to retell the ideas.

Adjectives	Nouns	Verbs
certain	behavior	confuse
likely	choice	depend on
perfect	decision	seem

1. Both writers discuss making decisions. In the first text, the writer talks about consumer's _____ . People are less _____ to buy something when there are more options. Having many choices _____ people. Other people think having more choices means you can find the _____ product. However, while it _____ like more choices would lead to more satisfaction, studies show fewer are better.

2. The second text talks about how people make _____ . People may show different _____ . Their decision may _____ on the type of purchase. However, most people belong in one of two groups. The first group wants to be _____ they are making the right choice. They do a lot of research. The second group makes fast decisions. In most cases, people in the second group are happier with their choice. The people in the first group are less certain they made the right choice.

B. Both writers ask readers to think about their behavior. Write sentences from each text that connect to the readers.

"Are More Choices Better?"	"Do Your Decisions Make You Happy?"

C. Compare your answers from Activity B with a partner. Then discuss which text is more likely to have an effect on your behavior.

Word Partners

case by case

in case of

in most cases

in some cases

rare cases

_____

GO ONLINE
to practice
word partners
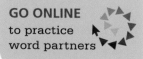

● Make Connections: Text to World

A. Do you agree with the results from the research studies? List examples to support your opinion. Look at the Oxford 2000 keywords on page 133 and find five words to help you.

1. I *agree   disagree* with the writer of "Are More Choices Better?"

   a. For example, _____

   _____

   b. For example, _____

   _____

2. I *agree   disagree* with "Do Your Decisions Make You Happy?"

   a. For example, _____

   _____

   b. For example, _____

B. Discuss your answers from Activity A with a partner.

C. Both texts show results from studies. How might people change their behavior based on the results? Read each situation, and then write a solution for the problem.

1. A new business is trying to sell coffee cups painted by new artists. It has a website that shows 50 different cups available, but the business is not doing well. What can you tell the owners to help their business? _____

   _____

   _____

2. A friend can't make a decision about which laptop to buy. She has done a lot of research and talked to many of her friends, but she still isn't certain. What can you tell her to help her? _____

   _____

   _____

Chant

GO ONLINE for the Chapter 8 Vocabulary & Grammar Chant

CHAPTER 9

How Does Nature Affect Us?

- Two vowels can make one sound
- Understand words that create cohesion
- Take notes and mark the text
- *which* and *which means that; even though* and *even when*

▲ BEFORE READING ▶ Oxford 2000 ✔ words to talk about nature and its effect on us

Learn Vocabulary

A. Read the definitions and look at the picture. Complete the paragraph with the bold words from the box.

air: the gases on earth that you breathe with your nose and mouth	**nature:** the plants and animals in the world
improve: to become better	**snow:** soft, white pieces of frozen water that fall from the sky when it is cold
mountain: a very high hill	**stress:** a bad feeling because of problems in life

At the park, there are trees, flowers, tables, and benches for people to sit and enjoy

_____ . Nature includes the plants and animals in the world. Land, like this tall

_____ , is part of nature, and so is the _____ that covers the top of the

mountain. People enjoy being in nature. They climb mountains and take walks in parks. They breathe the

fresh _____ . They have less _____ . As a result, they feel good. Nature

can _____ people's lives.

B. Match each picture to the correct sentence.

_____ Snow **breaks loose** from the top of a mountain and slides, or moves down.

_____ The snow **buried** my car.

__1__ The Earth is made of **layers** of rock.

_____ We have **extreme** weather with heavy rains and strong winds in hurricane season.

1.

2.

3.

4.

Oxford 2000 🔑

Use the Oxford 2000 list on page 133 to find more words to describe the pictures on these pages. Share your words with a partner.

C. Answer the questions with a partner.

1. Do you have **extreme** weather where you live?

2. What causes you to have **stress**?

3. When you feel **stress**, what do you do? How do you **improve** how you feel?

4. Circle the things that have different **layers**. With a partner, discuss what the layers are.

   cake   clothes   table   earth   chair

5. How does being in **nature** make you feel?

GO ONLINE
for more practice

Preview the Text

D. Look at the pictures on page 124. Answer the questions.

1. What is an *avalanche*? _____

_____

2. How do you think an airbag can help someone in an avalanche? _____

_____

3. What do you think happens to people in an avalanche? _____

_____

E. Look at the text on page 124. Circle the correct answer.

1. What will the writer NOT do?

   a. give steps for how to do something

   b. explain why something happens

   c. share a personal story

3. Read this sentence and tell what *it* refers to: "Because the snow builds up so quickly and is so heavy, the layers under *it* can weaken and break."

   a. snow   b. heavy   c. layers

2. The opposite feeling of *stress* is *calm*. The opposite meaning of *survive* is *die*. Which pair of words from the text have opposite meanings?

   a. heavy; weak

   b. ice; snow

   c. under; above

Sounds of English

Spelling Connection

A. Sometimes two vowels create one sound. Listen to the word *weather*. Do you hear the /ɛ/? Listen to each word below. What sound do the underlined vowels make? Write the word in the correct column.

<u>ai</u>r   br<u>ea</u>k   l<u>oo</u>se   m<u>ou</u>ntain   th<u>ou</u>gh

/aʊ/	/eɪ/	/ɛɾ/	/oʊ/	/u/

B. These words are in the text on page 124. Match the underlined vowels to the correct sound.

1. _____ danger<u>ou</u>s   a. /ɛ/

2. _____ d<u>ea</u>dly   b. /oʊ/

3. _____ snowb<u>oa</u>rding   c. /ʌ/

4. _____ br<u>ea</u>the   d. /eɪ/

5. _____ str<u>ai</u>ght   e. /i/

● Make Connections: Text to Self

A. Think of a time you were in extreme weather. Answer the questions.

1. What was the weather like? _____

_____

2. Why was it extreme? _____

_____

3. Did you feel stress? Why or why not? _____

_____

4. What did you do to feel safe? _____

_____

5. What can you tell someone to help him or her in extreme weather? _____

_____

B. Think about snow on a mountain. Complete the web.

C. Your best friend is going skiing on a large mountain. Give him or her some
   tips for how to be safe. Look at the pictures on page 124 and use your own
   ideas.

1. _____

2. _____

3. _____

▲▲ **DURING READING**
► Vocabulary strategy: Understand words that create cohesion
► Reading strategy: Take notes and mark the text

◀) Reading 1

A. Listen to how the reader emphasizes ideas and shows relationships in the text.

How to Survive an Avalanche

An avalanche is **snow** that travels fast down a **mountain**. The snow may also have ice and rocks in it. All avalanches are dangerous, but some are deadly. They depend on the amount of snow that **breaks loose** and slides. Avalanches kill about 150 people each year. Most people who die were out having fun in the snow, skiing or snowboarding. Often the cause of the avalanche is the movements, even small movements, of people on the mountain. Their movements cause the snow to shake and slide. How likely the snow is to slide depends on the weather. Most avalanches happen within 24 hours after a heavy snow. Because the snow builds up so quickly and is so heavy, the **layers** of ice and snow under it can weaken. Then they break. All it takes is a movement from a skier or other person on the mountain and the snow races downward. It can go as fast as a speeding car, which is about 80 miles per hour.

This skier has an airbag that will inflate in an avalanche.

If you are going to survive an avalanche, the most important time is at the beginning. This is when the snow begins to break apart. If you are skiing, try going straight down the mountain. Get as much speed as possible. Then move out of the way of the crashing snow. If you can't get away fast enough, look for any trees to grab, or hold onto. If you find yourself in the speeding snow, swim. Move your arms and legs as fast as you can. Try to stay above the snow. The most important thing is not to get **buried** under the snow. Only one in four people completely buried survives. The snow gets heavier as it comes to a stop and settles on the mountain. The human body is heavier than the snow and will sink under the snow unless you fight to stay above it.

People can survive avalanches. In fact, even though some people were buried, they still survived. They have shared their stories and their rules for staying alive. First, carry the right equipment. Buy a small radio that sends signals so people can find you. Bring an airbag with you. You carry this on your back, and in an avalanche it fills with **air**, which helps keep you from being buried under the heavy snow. This will make it easier for people to find you. Second, cover your mouth with your hands. You need to make room for air. Most people who don't survive an avalanche die because they can't breathe in the snow. Finally, stay calm. People can survive the most **extreme** weather. If you can think calmly, then you can make your next move.

In an avalanche, snow slides down a mountain, burying everything in its path.

Stop and Think

How will holding onto a tree in an avalanche help you? Make an inference.

B. Read the text aloud. Slow down to stress contrasts, surprising ideas, and interesting facts.

Check Your Understanding

C. Complete the outline with ideas from the text on page 124.

I. Avalanches

  A. Causes

    1. <u>movement of a person on a mountain</u>

    2. _____

  B. Surviving an avalanche at the beginning

    1. Ski straight down the mountain and get out of the way.

    2. Look for _____ .

    3. _____

      a. Snow gets heavier as _____ .

      b. The human body will _____ .

  C. People can survive if buried

    1. _____

      a. Buy _____ .

      b. Bring _____ .

    2. _____

    3. _____

Vocabulary Strategy

Understand Words That Create Cohesion

Writers use words to talk about a topic and connect the ideas. This is called *cohesion*. Look for the following to identify and understand the ideas in a text.

1. Look for synonyms the writers uses to discuss the topic.

The writer uses these words for speed: *travels fast, race.*

2. Look at the pronouns. What do they refer to?

   The <u>snow</u> races downward. **It** can go as fast as a speeding car, which is about 80 miles per hour.

The writer uses *it* to refer to *snow.*

3. Notice that the writer leaves out some words. You must think of them yourself.

   <u>The snow</u> gets heavier as **it** comes to a stop and settles on the mountain.

4. Look for signal words (*first, next, then*) and conjunctions (*and, but, or*). How do they connect ideas?

GO ONLINE
for more
practice

D. Read the text on page 124 again. Answer the questions.

1. What is a synonym for *staying alive*? _____

2. What does the pronoun *they* refer to in the first paragraph?

   _____

   What does *they* refer to in the last paragraph? _____

3. What does *this* refer to in the sentence *You carry this on your back*?

   _____

4. *The human body is heavier than the snow and will sink unless you fight to stay above the snow.* What will sink? _____

GO ONLINE
for more
practice

Reading Strategy

Take Notes and Mark the Text

Take notes and mark the text to help you understand and remember the ideas. Use these tips.

1. Highlight or underline the main idea in each paragraph.
2. Number the supporting ideas, steps, or examples that support the main idea.
3. Circle any words or ideas you don't understand so you can reread to figure out their meaning.
4. Label any relationships in the text, such as words and definitions, cause-effect, comparison, and contrasts.
5. Write any ideas or questions you have in the margin next to the text.

E. Follow each direction from the Reading Strategy box to mark the text for paragraphs 2 and 3 in the text on page 124.

🔊 Reading 2

A. Preview the text. Then read it to yourself.

Do We Need Nature?

People at this hotel can enjoy the pool and beautiful view in the Sky Park.

Cities cover 2 to 3 percent of the world. The number of people moving to cities is growing, and cities themselves are getting bigger, replacing forests and farmland. Some researchers predict that by 2030, 10 percent of the world's land will be covered by cities. People in cities spend much more of their time inside and much less of their time around **nature**. This affects how they feel and even think. For instance, people who live near parks have less **stress**. In addition, studies have shown that a simple walk in nature makes people happier. Another study supports this. It showed that the part of the brain involved with negative thinking is less active after walking through nature. In contrast, people who walked through an urban area near a highway did not have the same results. Being in nature actually changes the way the brain works.

The natural world seems to be connected to our human nature. People in every culture choose to look at pictures of nature. In fact, simply looking at nature has positive effects. After one hour in nature, workers **improved** how long they could concentrate by 20 percent. In offices that have views of nature, employees are sick less often. In addition, people in the hospital who had views of a tree had shorter hospital stays and reported less pain than those whose windows looked at other buildings, which means that nature greatly affects us. If we can find ways to make nature part of our increasingly urban lives, then we can be healthier.

One solution is to design cities to look like nature. This is actually happening in some places. People relax under palm trees from more than 650 feet in the **air**. Where are they?

On a **mountain**? No, the people enjoying the view are in the Sky Park in a hotel in Singapore. The architects designed this park to look like the natural world. There are trees next to water and a big open sky above.

Another solution is to bring nature to the city. People all over the world are planting gardens and creating park spaces in cities. In New York City and Chicago, planners turned old railway lines into parks. People are giving nature a home in cities, and some animals are making their homes there too. Peregrine falcons have moved from high cliffs in forests to cities. They have adapted to their new environment. They make their homes on tall buildings. They eat other birds and small animals on the city streets. Songbirds now sing louder in cities so they can be heard over the traffic, which means that the natural world is changing. Even when cities grow, nature can too.

The High Line is a park in New York City that used to be a railway line for trains.

Stop and Think

Can we build cities to look like nature? What do you think? Will they have the same effect on us?

Grammar in the Readings

Notice *which* and *which means that* in the readings.

Use a comma and *which* to add a comment that explains a whole sentence.

> You carry this on your back and in an avalanche it fills with air, **which** <u>helps keep you from being buried under the heavy snow</u>.

Use a comma and *which means that* to introduce a complete sentence.

> Songbirds now sing louder in cities so they can be heard over the traffic, **which means that** <u>the natural world is changing</u>.

Notice *even though* and *even when* in the readings.

Use *even though* and *even when* to introduce an idea that is surprising.

> In fact, **even though** some people were buried, they still survived.
> **Even when** cities grow, nature can too.

GO ONLINE
for grammar practice

Check Your Understanding

B. Complete the webs with ideas from the text on pages 126–127.

1. What are examples of the natural world?

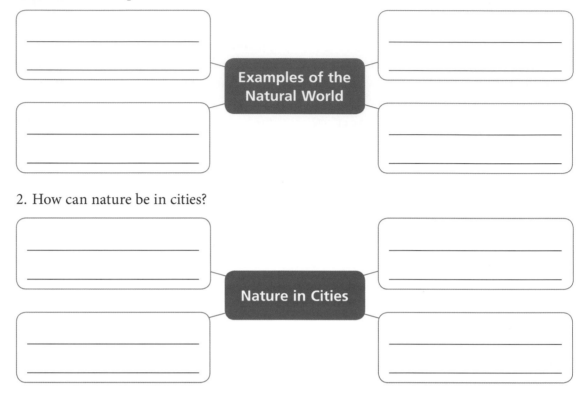

Examples of the Natural World

2. How can nature be in cities?

Nature in Cities

Vocabulary Strategy: Understand Words That Create Cohesion

C. Read the text on pages 126–127 again. Answer the questions.

1. What is a synonym for *city*? _____

2. The writer refers to nature. She talks about parks and the

_____ world.

3. What idea does *this* refer to in the sentence *This affects how they feel and even think?*

_____

4. *Even when cities grow, nature can too.* Nature can do what?

_____

Reading Strategy: Take Notes and Mark the Text

D. Follow the directions to mark the text on pages 126–127. Then compare your notes with a partner.

1. Highlight a sentence that is the main idea of paragraph 2.

2. Number three examples to support the main idea in paragraph 2.

3. Label a sentence that uses cause-effect in paragraph 2.

4. Write a question about the text in the margin.

● **Make Connections:** Text to Text

A. Both writers discuss the effect of nature on people. How does each text describe nature? Complete the Venn diagram.

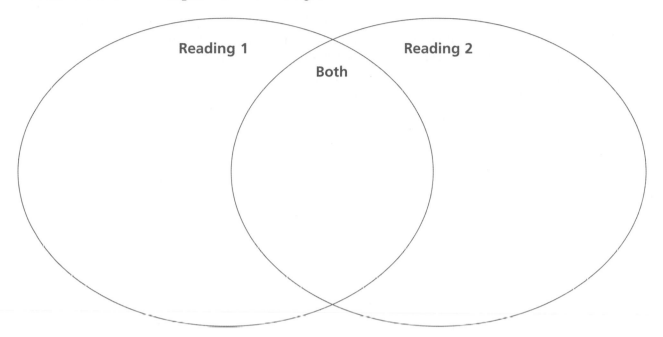

B. The writers use the phrases *even though* and *even when* to introduce something surprising. Complete the sentences below using ideas you learned from the two texts.

1. Even when someone is buried in snow, _____

_____

2. Even though cities are getting bigger, _____

_____

3. Even though the human body is heavier than snow, _____

_____

4. Even when people went for a walk in an urban area, _____

_____

C. Both writers use *if* statements to discuss what can happen. Summarize each text with an *if* statement.

Reading 1: If you are in an avalanche, _____

_____

Reading 2: If cities grow, _____

_____

Summarizing and Retelling

A. Complete the sentences with the words from the box. Some of the words have to be changed to fit the sentences. For example, *layer* has to be changed to *layers*. Then read the questions and answers to a partner to retell the ideas.

Adjectives	Nouns		Verbs
extreme	air	nature	break
	layer	snow	bury
	mountain	stress	improve

1. What causes avalanches?

   A person's movement on a(n) _____ causes snow and ice to

   _____ loose. The _____ under the new snow weaken.

   This is more likely to happen after _____ weather, like a lot of snow.

2. What should you do if you are in an avalanche?

   Try to get down the mountain as fast as possible. Move out of the way so you don't get

   _____ in the _____, which makes it difficult to find you.

3. What should I take with me when I ski?

   Bring an airbag. The _____ in the bag will help you in an avalanche so

   you don't get buried. Also take a radio so people can find you if you do get buried.

4. Why do people spend less time in nature?

   Many people live in cities, and as a result, they work inside more and see

   _____ less.

5. Why do we need nature?

   A walk in a park changes the way the brain works. Being in nature _____

   how we think. People feel better and have less _____ after a walk through

   a park.

B. What other questions does each text answer? List questions for each text. Then take turns asking and answering them with a partner.

"How to Survive an Avalanche"	"Do We Need Nature?"

Word Partners

be under stress

cause stress

high stress

low stress

manage stress

GO ONLINE
to practice
word partners

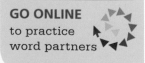

⬤ **Make Connections:** Text to World

A. Think about the ideas from the two texts. What other ideas can you add? Look at the Oxford 2000 words on page 133 and find three words to help you.

In "How to Survive an Avalanche" the writer gives tips. List other tips you think might help.

1. Swim so you don't sink in the snow.

2. _____

3. _____

In "Do We Need Nature?" the writer gives examples for bringing nature to cities. List your own examples.

1. People plant gardens in cities.

2. _____

3. _____

B. In "Do We Need Nature?" the writer explains the positive effects of nature on people. Do you agree that nature makes people feel better? Why or why not? List examples to support your opinion.

1. _____

2. _____

3. _____

C. Sometimes when you read a text, it makes you think of related ideas or questions. What do these texts make you think of?

Why do people do dangerous sports like skiing?	**"How to Survive an Avalanche"**	_____
_____		_____

Will cities in the future look more like the natural world?	**"Do We Need Nature?"**	_____
_____		_____

Chant

GO ONLINE for the Chapter 9 Vocabulary & Grammar Chant

Look at the word bank for Unit 3. Check (✓) the words you know.
Circle the words you want to learn better.

OXFORD 2000 🔑				
Adjectives	**Nouns**		**Verbs**	
certain	air	solution	break	seem (like)
extreme	behavior	stress	bury	solve
huge	choice	tool	confuse	survive
intelligent	decision		depend (on)	
likely	layer		ignore	
loose	mountain		improve	
perfect	nature		list	
	problem		refer (to)	
	snow		search	

PRACTICE WITH THE OXFORD 2000 🔑

A. Use the words in the chart. Match adjectives with nouns.

1. _____perfect solution_____ 2. _____

3. _____ 4. _____

5. _____

B. Use the words in the chart. Match verbs with nouns.

1. _____ignore the problem_____ 2. _____

3. _____ 4. _____

5. _____

C. Use the words in the chart. Match verbs with adjective noun partners.

1. _seem like a huge decision_ 2. _____

3. _____ 4. _____

5. _____

THE OXFORD 2000 ⚷ LIST OF KEYWORDS

This is a list of the 2000 most important and useful words to learn at this stage in your language learning. These words have been carefully chosen by a group of language experts and experienced teachers, who have judged the words to be important and useful for three reasons.

- Words that are used very **frequently** (= very often) in English are included in this list. Frequency information has been gathered from the American English section of the Oxford English Corpus, which is a collection of written and spoken texts containing over 2 billion words.

- The keywords are frequent across a **range** of different types of text. This means that the keywords are often used in a variety of contexts, not just in newspapers or in scientific articles for example.

- The list includes some important words which are very **familiar** to most users of English, even though they are not used very frequently. These include, for example, words which are useful for explaining what you mean when you do not know the exact word for something.

Names of people, places, etc. beginning with a capital letter are not included in the list of 2000 keywords. Keywords which are not included in the list are numbers, days of the week, and the months of the year.

A

a, an *indefinite article*
ability *n.*
able *adj.*
about *adv., prep.*
above *prep., adv.*
absolutely *adv.*
academic *adj.*
accept *v.*
acceptable *adj.*
accident *n.*
  by accident
according to prep.
account *n.*
accurate *adj.*
accuse *v.*
achieve *v.*
achievement *n.*
acid *n.*
across *adv., prep.*
act *n., v.*
action *n.*
active *adj.*
activity *n.*
actor, actress *n.*
actual *adj.*
actually *adv.*
add *v.*
address *n.*
admire *v.*
admit *v.*
adult *n.*
advanced *adj.*
advantage *n.*
adventure *n.*
advertisement *n.*
advice *n.*

advise *v.*
affect *v.*
afford *v.*
afraid *adj.*
after *prep., conj., adv.*
afternoon *n.*
afterward *adv.*
again *adv.*
against *prep.*
age *n.*
  aged *adj.*
ago *adv.*
agree *v.*
agreement *n.*
ahead *adv.*
aim *n., v.*
air *n.*
airplane *n.*
airport *n.*
alarm *n.*
alcohol *n.*
alcoholic *adj.*
alive *adj.*
all *adj., pron., adv.*
allow *v.*
all right *adj., adv., exclamation*
almost *adv.*
alone *adj., adv.*
along *prep., adv.*
alphabet *n.*
already *adv.*
also *adv.*
although *conj.*
always *adv.*
among *prep.*
amount *n.*

amuse *v.*
analyze *v.*
analysis *n.*
ancient *adj.*
and *conj.*
anger *n.*
angle *n.*
angry *adj.*
animal *n.*
announce *v.*
another *adj., pron.*
answer *n., v.*
any *adj., pron., adv.*
anymore *(also* any more*)* *adv.*
anyone *(also* anybody*)* *pron.*
anything *pron.*
anyway *adv.*
anywhere *adv.*
apart *adv.*
apartment *n.*
apparently *adv.*
appear *v.*
appearance *n.*
apple *n.*
apply *v.*
appointment *n.*
appreciate *v.*
appropriate *adj.*
approve *v.*
area *n.*
argue *v.*
argument *n.*
arm *n.*
army *n.*
around *adv., prep.*

arrange *v.*
arrangement *n.*
arrest *v.*
arrive *v.*
arrow *n.*
art *n.*
article *n.*
artificial *adj.*
artist *n.*
artistic *adj.*
as *prep., conj.*
ashamed *adj.*
ask *v.*
asleep *adj.*
at *prep.*
atmosphere *n.*
atom *n.*
attach *v.*
attack *n., v.*
attention *n.*
attitude *n.*
attract *v.*
attractive *adj.*
aunt *n.*
authority *n.*
available *adj.*
average *adj., n.*
avoid *v.*
awake *adj.*
aware *adj.*
away *adv.*

B

baby *n.*
back *n., adj., adv.*
backward *adv.*
bad *adj.*

badly *adv.*
bag *n.*
bake *v.*
balance *n.*
ball *n.*
band *n.*
bank *n.*
bar *n.*
base *n., v.*
baseball *n.*
basic *adj.*
basis *n.*
bath *n.*
bathroom *n.*
be *v.*
beach *n.*
bear *v.*
beard *n.*
beat *v.*
beautiful *adj.*
beauty *n.*
because *conj.*
become *v.*
bed *n.*
bedroom *n.*
beer *n.*
before *prep., conj., adv.*
begin *v.*
beginning *n.*
behave *v.*
behavior *n.*
behind *prep., adv.*
belief *n.*
believe *v.*
bell *n.*
belong *v.*
below *prep., adv.*
belt *n.*
bend *v.*
benefit *n.*
beside *prep.*
best *adj., adv., n.*
better *adj., adv.*
between *prep., adv.*
beyond *prep., adv.*
bicycle *n.*
big *adj.*
bill *n.*
bird *n.*
birth *n.*
birthday *n.*
bite *v.*
bitter *adj.*
black *adj.*
blame *v.*
block *n.*
blood *n.*
blow *v., n.*
blue *adj., n.*

board *n.*
boat *n.*
body *n.*
boil *v.*
bomb *n., v.*
bone *n.*
book *n.*
boot *n.*
border *n.*
bored *adj.*
boring *adj.*
born: be born *v.*
borrow *v.*
boss *n.*
both *adj., pron.*
bother *v.*
bottle *n.*
bottom *n.*
bowl *n.*
box *n.*
boy *n.*
boyfriend *n.*
brain *n.*
branch *n.*
brave *adj.*
bread *n.*
break *v.*
breakfast *n.*
breath *n.*
breathe *v.*
brick *n.*
bridge *n.*
brief *adj.*
bright *adj.*
bring *v.*
broken *adj.*
brother *n.*
brown *adj., n.*
brush *n., v.*
bubble *n.*
build *v.*
building *n.*
bullet *n.*
burn *v.*
burst *v.*
bury *v.*
bus *n.*
bush *n.*
business *n.*
busy *adj.*
but *conj.*
butter *n.*
button *n.*
buy *v.*
by *prep.*
bye *exclamation*

C

cabinet *n.*

cake *n.*
calculate *v.*
call *v., n.*
calm *adj.*
camera *n.*
camp *n., v.*
can *modal v., n.*
cancel *v.*
candy *n.*
capable *adj.*
capital *n.*
car *n.*
card *n.*
care *n., v.*
   take care of
   care for
career *n.*
careful *adj.*
carefully *adv.*
careless *adj.*
carelessly *adv.*
carry *v.*
case *n.*
   in case (of)
cash *n.*
cat *n.*
catch *v.*
cause *n., v.*
CD *n.*
ceiling *n.*
celebrate *v.*
cell *n.*
cell phone *n.*
cent *n.*
center *n.*
centimeter *n.*
central *adj.*
century *n.*
ceremony *n.*
certain *adj.*
certainly *adv.*
chain *n., v.*
chair *n.*
challenge *n.*
chance *n.*
change *v., n.*
character *n.*
characteristic *n.*
charge *n., v.*
charity *n.*
chase *v., n.*
cheap *adj.*
cheat *v.*
check *v., n.*
cheek *n.*
cheese *n.*
chemical *adj., n.*
chemistry *n.*
chest *n.*

chicken *n.*
chief *adj., n.*
child *n.*
childhood *n.*
chin *n.*
chocolate *n.*
choice *n.*
choose *v.*
church *n.*
cigarette *n.*
circle *n.*
citizen *n.*
city *n.*
class *n.*
clean *adj., v.*
clear *adj., v.*
clearly *adv.*
climate *n.*
climb *v.*
clock *n.*
close /kloʊs/ *adj., adv.*
close /kloʊz/ *v.*
closed *adj.*
cloth *n.*
clothes *n.*
clothing *n.*
cloud *n.*
club *n.*
coast *n.*
coat *n.*
coffee *n.*
coin *n.*
cold *adj., n.*
collect *v.*
collection *n.*
college *n.*
color *n., v.*
column *n.*
combination *n.*
combine *v.*
come *v.*
comfortable *adj.*
command *n.*
comment *n., v.*
common *adj.*
communicate *v.*
communication *n.*
community *n.*
company *n.*
compare *v.*
comparison *n.*
competition *n.*
complain *v.*
complaint *n.*
complete *adj.*
completely *adv.*
complicated *adj.*
computer *n.*
concentrate *v.*

concert *n.*
conclusion *n.*
condition *n.*
confidence *n.*
confident *adj.*
confuse *v.*
confused *adj.*
connect *v.*
connection *n.*
conscious *adj.*
consider *v.*
consist *v.*
constant *adj.*
contact *n., v.*
contain *v.*
container *n.*
continent *n.*
continue *v.*
continuous *adj.*
contract *n.*
contrast *n.*
contribute *v.*
control *n., v.*
convenient *adj.*
conversation *n.*
convince *v.*
cook *v.*
cookie *n.*
cooking *n.*
cool *adj.*
copy *n., v.*
corner *n.*
correct *adj., v.*
correctly *adv.*
cost *n., v.*
cotton *n.*
cough *v.*
could *modal v.*
count *v.*
country *n.*
county *n.*
couple *n.*
course *n.*
   of course
court *n.*
cousin *n.*
cover *v., n.*
covering *n.*
cow *n.*
crack *v.*
crash *n., v.*
crazy *adj.*
cream *n., adj.*
create *v.*
credit card *n.*
crime *n.*
criminal *adj., n.*
crisis *n.*
criticism *n.*

criticize *v.*
cross *v.*
crowd *n.*
cruel *adj.*
crush *v.*
cry *v.*
culture *n.*
cup *n.*
curly *adj.*
curve *n.*
curved *adj.*
custom *n.*
customer *n.*
cut *v., n.*

D
dad *n.*
damage *n., v.*
dance *n., v.*
dancer *n.*
danger *n.*
dangerous *adj.*
dark *adj., n.*
date *n.*
daughter *n.*
day *n.*
dead *adj.*
deal *v.*
dear *adj.*
death *n.*
debt *n.*
decide *v.*
decision *n.*
decorate *v.*
deep *adj.*
deeply *adv.*
defeat *v.*
definite *adj.*
definitely *adv.*
definition *n.*
degree *n.*
deliberately *adv.*
deliver *v.*
demand *n., v.*
dentist *n.*
deny *v.*
department *n.*
depend *v.*
depression *n.*
describe *v.*
description *n.*
desert *n.*
deserve *v.*
design *n., v.*
desk *n.*
despite *prep.*
destroy *v.*
detail *n.*
   in detail

determination *n.*
determined *adj.*
develop *v.*
development *n.*
device *n.*
diagram *n.*
dictionary *n.*
die *v.*
difference *n.*
different *adj.*
difficult *adj.*
difficulty *n.*
dig *v.*
dinner *n.*
direct *adj., adv., v.*
direction *n.*
directly *adv.*
dirt *n.*
dirty *adj.*
disadvantage *n.*
disagree *v.*
disagreement *n.*
disappear *v.*
disappoint *v.*
disaster *n.*
discover *v.*
discuss *v.*
discussion *n.*
disease *n.*
disgusting *adj.*
dish *n.*
dishonest *adj.*
disk *n.*
distance *n.*
distant *adj.*
disturb *v.*
divide *v.*
division *n.*
divorce *n., v.*
do *v., auxiliary v.*
doctor *n.* (*abbr.* Dr.)
document *n.*
dog *n.*
dollar *n.*
door *n.*
dot *n.*
double *adj.*
doubt *n.*
down *adv., prep.*
downstairs *adv., adj.*
downward *adv.*
draw *v.*
drawer *n.*
drawing *n*
dream *n., v.*
dress *n., v.*
drink *n., v.*
drive *v., n.*
driver *n.*

drop *v., n.*
drug *n.*
dry *adj., v.*
during *prep.*
dust *n.*
duty *n.*
DVD *n.*

E
each *adj., pron.*
each other *pron.*
ear *n.*
early *adj., adv.*
earn *v.*
earth *n.*
easily *adv.*
east *n., adj., adv.*
eastern *adj.*
easy *adj.*
eat *v.*
economic *adj.*
economy *n.*
edge *n.*
educate *v.*
education *n.*
effect *n.*
effort *n.*
e.g. *abbr.*
egg *n.*
either *adj., pron., adv.*
election *n.*
electric *adj.*
electrical *adj.*
electricity *n.*
electronic *adj.*
else *adv.*
e-mail (*also* email) *n., v.*
embarrass *v.*
embarrassed *adj.*
emergency *n.*
emotion *n.*
employ *v.*
employment *n.*
empty *adj.*
encourage *v.*
end *n., v.*
   in the end
enemy *n.*
energy *n.*
engine *n.*
enjoy *v.*
enjoyable *adj.*
enjoyment *n.*
enough *adj., pron., adv.*
enter *v.*
entertain *v.*
entertainment *n.*
enthusiasm *n.*
enthusiastic *adj.*

The Oxford 2000 List of Keywords

entrance n.
environment n.
equal adj.
equipment n.
error n.
escape v.
especially adv.
essential adj.
etc. abbr.
even adv.
evening n.
event n.
ever adv.
every adj.
everybody pron.
everyone pron.
everything pron.
everywhere adv.
evidence n.
evil adj.
exact adj.
exactly adv.
exaggerate v.
exam n.
examination n.
examine v.
example n.
excellent adj.
except prep.
exchange v., n.
excited adj.
excitement n.
exciting adj.
excuse n., v.
exercise n.
exist v.
exit n.
expect v.
expensive adj.
experience n., v.
experiment n.
expert n.
explain v.
explanation n.
explode v.
explore v.
explosion n.
expression n.
extra adj., adv.
extreme adj.
extremely adv.
eye n.

F
face n., v.
fact n.
factory n.
fail v.
failure n.

fair adj.
fall v., n.
false adj.
familiar adj.
family n.
famous adj.
far adv., adj.
farm n.
farmer n.
fashion n.
fashionable adj.
fast adj., adv.
fasten v.
fat adj., n.
father n.
fault n.
favor n.
    in favor
favorite adj., n.
fear n., v.
feather n.
feature n.
feed v.
feel v.
feeling n.
female adj.
fence n.
festival n.
few adj., pron.
    a few
field n.
fight v., n.
figure n.
file n.
fill v.
film n.
final adj.
finally adv.
financial adj.
find v.
    find out sth
fine adj.
finger n.
finish v.
fire n., v.
firm n., adj.
firmly adv.
first adj., adv., n.
    at first
fish n.
fit v., adj.
fix v.
fixed adj.
flag n.
flame n.
flash v.
flat adj.
flavor n.
flight n.

float v.
flood n.
floor n.
flour n.
flow v.
flower n.
fly v.
fold v.
follow v.
food n.
foot n.
football n.
for prep.
force n., v.
foreign adj.
forest n.
forever adv.
forget v.
forgive v.
fork n.
form n., v.
formal adj.
forward adv.
frame n.
free adj., v., adv.
freedom n.
freeze v.
fresh adj.
friend n.
friendly adj.
friendship n.
frighten v.
from prep.
front n., adj.
    in front
frozen adj.
fruit n.
fry v.
fuel n.
full adj.
fully adv.
fun n., adj.
funny adj.
fur n.
furniture n.
further adj., adv.
future n., adj.

G
gain v.
gallon n.
game n.
garbage n.
garden n.
gas n.
gate n.
general adj.
    in general
generally adv.

generous adj.
gentle adj.
gently adv.
gentleman n.
get v.
gift n.
girl n.
girlfriend n.
give v.
glass n.
glasses n.
global adj.
glove n.
go v.
goal n.
god n.
gold n., adj.
good adj., n.
goodbye exclamation
goods n.
govern v.
government n.
grade n., v.
grain n.
gram n.
grammar n.
grandchild n.
grandfather n.
grandmother n.
grandparent n.
grass n.
grateful adj.
gray adj., n.
great adj.
green adj., n.
groceries n.
ground n.
group n.
grow v.
growth n.
guard n., v.
guess v.
guest n.
guide n.
guilty adj.
gun n.

H
habit n.
hair n.
half n., adj., pron., adv.
hall n.
hammer n.
hand n.
handle v., n.
hang v.
happen v.
happiness n.
happy adj.

hard *adj., adv.*
hardly *adv.*
harm *n., v.*
harmful *adj.*
hat *n.*
hate *v., n.*
have *v.*
    have to *modal v.*
he *pron.*
head *n.*
health *n.*
healthy *adj.*
hear *v.*
heart *n.*
heat *n., v.*
heavy *adj.*
height *n.*
hello *exclamation*
help *v., n.*
helpful *adj.*
her *pron., adj.*
here *adv.*
hers *pron.*
herself *pron.*
hide *v.*
high *adj., adv.*
highly *adv.*
high school *n.*
highway *n.*
hill *n.*
him *pron.*
himself *pron.*
hire *v.*
his *adj., pron.*
history *n.*
hit *v., n.*
hold *v., n.*
hole *n.*
holiday *n.*
home *n., adv..*
honest *adj.*
hook *n.*
hope *v., n.*
horn *n.*
horse *n.*
hospital *n.*
hot *adj.*
hotel *n.*
hour *n.*
house *n.*
how *adv.*
however *adv.*
huge *adj.*
human *adj., n.*
humor *n.*
hungry *adj.*
hunt *v.*
hurry *v., n.*
hurt *v.*

husband *n.*

I

I *pron.*
ice *n.*
idea *n.*
identify *v.*
if *conj.*
ignore *v.*
illegal *adj.*
illegally *adv.*
illness *n.*
image *n.*
imagination *n.*
imagine *v.*
immediate *adj.*
immediately *adv.*
impatient *adj.*
importance *n.*
important *adj.*
impossible *adj.*
impress *v.*
impression *n.*
improve *v.*
improvement *n.*
in *prep., adv.*
inch *n.*
include *v.*
including *prep.*
increase *v., n.*
indeed *adv.*
independent *adj.*
individual *adj.*
industry *n.*
infection *n.*
influence *n.*
inform *v.*
informal *adj.*
information *n.*
injure *v.*
injury *n.*
insect *n.*
inside *prep., adv., n., adj.*
instead *adv., prep.*
instruction *n.*
instrument *n.*
insult *v., n.*
intelligent *adj.*
intend *v.*
intention *n.*
interest *n., v.*
interested *adj.*
interesting *adj.*
international *adj.*
Internet *n.*
interrupt *v.*
interview *n.*
into *prep.*
introduce *v.*

introduction *n.*
invent *v.*
investigate *v.*
invitation *n.*
invite *v.*
involve *v.*
iron *n.*
island *n.*
issue *n.*
it *pron.*
item *n.*
its *adj.*
itself *pron.*

J

jacket *n.*
jeans *n.*
jewelry *n.*
job *n.*
join *v.*
joke *n., v.*
judge *n., v.*
judgment *(also*
    judgement) *n.*
juice *n.*
jump *v.*
just *adv.*

K

keep *v.*
key *n.*
kick *v., n.*
kid *n., v.*
kill *v.*
kilogram *(also* kilo) *n.*
kilometer *n.*
kind *n., adj.*
kindness *n.*
king *n.*
kiss *v., n.*
kitchen *n.*
knee *n.*
knife *n.*
knock *v., n.*
knot *n.*
know *v.*
knowledge *n.*

L

lack *n.*
lady *n.*
lake *n.*
lamp *n.*
land *n., v.*
language *n.*
large *adj.*
last *adj., adv., n., v.*
late *adj., adv.*
later *adv.*

laugh *v.*
laundry *n.*
law *n.*
lawyer *n.*
lay *v.*
layer *n.*
lazy *adj.*
lead /lid/ *v.*
leader *n.*
leaf *n.*
lean *v.*
learn *v.*
least *adj., pron., adv.*
    at least
leather *n.*
leave *v.*
left *adj., adv., n.*
leg *n.*
legal *adj.*
legally *adv.*
lemon *n.*
lend *v.*
length *n.*
less *adj., pron., adv.*
lesson *n.*
let *v.*
letter *n.*
level *n.*
library *n.*
lid *n.*
lie *v., n.*
life *n.*
lift *v.*
light *n., adj., v.*
lightly *adv.*
like *prep., v., conj.*
likely *adj.*
limit *n., v.*
line *n.*
lip *n.*
liquid *n., adj.*
list *n., v.*
listen *v.*
liter *n.*
literature *n.*
little *adj., pron., adv.*
    a little
live /lɪv/ *v.*
living *adj.*
load *n., v.*
loan *n.*
local *adj.*
lock *v., n.*
lonely *adj.*
long *adj., adv.*
look *v., n.*
loose *adj.*
lose *v.*
loss *n.*

The Oxford 2000 List of Keywords

lost *adj.*
lot *pron., adv.*
  a lot (of)
  lots (of)
loud *adj.*
loudly *adv.*
love *n., v.*
low *adj., adv.*
luck *n.*
lucky *adj.*
lump *n.*
lunch *n.*

M

machine *n.*
magazine *n.*
magic *n., adj.*
mail *n., v.*
main *adj.*
mainly *adv.*
make *v.*
male *adj., n.*
man *n.*
manage *v.*
manager *n.*
many *adj., pron.*
map *n.*
mark *n., v.*
market *n.*
marriage *n.*
married *adj.*
marry *v.*
match *n., v.*
material *n.*
math *n.*
mathematics *n.*
matter *n., v.*
may *modal v.*
maybe *adv.*
me *pron.*
meal *n.*
mean *v.*
meaning *n.*
measure *v., n.*
measurement *n.*
meat *n.*
medical *adj.*
medicine *n.*
medium *adj.*
meet *v.*
meeting *n.*
melt *v.*
member *n.*
memory *n.*
mental *adj.*
mention *v.*
mess *n.*
message *n.*
messy *adj.*

metal *n.*
method *n.*
meter *n.*
middle *n., adj.*
midnight *n.*
might *modal v.*
mile *n.*
milk *n.*
mind *n., v.*
mine *pron.*
minute *n.*
mirror *n.*
Miss *n.*
miss *v.*
missing *adj.*
mistake *n.*
mix *v.*
mixture *n.*
model *n.*
modern *adj.*
mom *n.*
moment *n.*
money *n.*
month *n.*
mood *n.*
moon *n.*
moral *adj.*
morally *adv.*
more *adj., pron., adv.*
morning *n.*
most *adj., pron., adv.*
mostly *adv.*
mother *n.*
motorcycle *n.*
mountain *n.*
mouse *n.*
mouth *n.*
move *v., n.*
movement *n.*
movie *n.*
Mr. *abbr.*
Mrs. *abbr.*
Ms. *abbr.*
much *adj., pron., adv.*
mud *n.*
multiply *v.*
murder *n., v.*
muscle *n.*
museum *n.*
music *n.*
musical *adj.*
musician *n.*
must *modal v.*
my *adj.*
myself *pron.*
mysterious *adj.*

N

nail *n.*

name *n., v.*
narrow *adj.*
nation *n.*
national *adj.*
natural *adj.*
nature *n.*
navy *n.*
near *adj., adv., prep.*
nearby *adj., adv.*
nearly *adv.*
neat *adj.*
neatly *adv.*
necessary *adj.*
neck *n.*
need *v., n.*
needle *n.*
negative *adj.*
neighbor *n.*
neither *adj., pron., adv.*
nerve *n.*
nervous *adj.*
net *n.*
never *adv.*
new *adj.*
news *n.*
newspaper *n.*
next *adj., adv., n.*
nice *adj.*
night *n.*
no *exclamation, adj.*
nobody *pron.*
noise *n.*
noisy *adj.*
noisily *adv.*
none *pron.*
nonsense *n.*
no one *pron.*
nor *conj.*
normal *adj.*
normally *adv.*
north *n., adj., adv.*
northern *adj.*
nose *n.*
not *adv.*
note *n.*
nothing *pron.*
notice *v.*
novel *n.*
now *adv.*
nowhere *adv.*
nuclear *adj.*
number (*abbr.* No., no.) *n.*
nurse *n.*
nut *n.*

O

object *n.*
obtain *v.*
obvious *adj.*

occasion *n.*
occur *v.*
ocean *n.*
o'clock *adv.*
odd *adj.*
of *prep.*
off *adv., prep.*
offense *n.*
offer *v., n.*
office *n.*
officer *n.*
official *adj., n.*
officially *adv.*
often *adv.*
oh *exclamation*
oil *n.*
OK (*also* okay)
  exclamation, adj., adv.
old *adj.*
old-fashioned *adj.*
on *prep., adv.*
once *adv., conj.*
one *number, adj., pron.*
onion *n.*
only *adj., adv.*
onto *prep.*
open *adj., v..*
operate *v.*
operation *n.*
opinion *n.*
opportunity *n.*
opposite *adj., adv., n., prep.*
or *conj.*
orange *n., adj.*
order *n., v.*
ordinary *adj.*
organization *n.*
organize *v.*
organized *adj.*
original *adj., n.*
other *adj., pron.*
otherwise *adv.*
ought to *modal v.*
ounce *n.*
our *adj.*
ours *pron.*
ourselves *pron.*
out *adj., adv.*
out of *prep.*
outside *n., adj., prep., adv.*
oven *n.*
over *adv., prep.*
owe *v.*
own *adj., pron., v.*
owner *n.*

P

pack *v., n.*
package *n.*

page *n.*
pain *n.*
painful *adj.*
paint *n., v.*
painter *n.*
painting *n.*
pair *n.*
pale *adj.*
pan *n.*
pants *n.*
paper *n.*
parent *n.*
park *n., v.*
part *n.*
   take part (in)
particular *adj.*
particularly *adv.*
partly *adv.*
partner *n.*
party *n.*
pass *v.*
passage *n.*
passenger *n.*
passport *n.*
past *adj., n., prep., adv.*
path *n.*
patient *n., adj.*
pattern *n.*
pause *v.*
pay *v., n.*
payment *n.*
peace *n.*
peaceful *adj.*
pen *n.*
pencil *n.*
people *n.*
perfect *adj.*
perform *v.*
performance *n.*
perhaps *adv.*
period *n.*
permanent *adj.*
permission *n.*
person *n.*
personal *adj.*
personality *n.*
persuade *v.*
pet *n.*
phone *n.*
photo *n.*
photograph *n.*
phrase *n.*
physical *adj.*
physically *adv.*
piano *n.*
pick *v.*
   pick sth up
picture *n.*
piece *n.*

pig *n.*
pile *n.*
pilot *n.*
pin *n.*
pink *adj., n.*
pint *n.*
pipe *n.*
place *n., v.*
   take place
plain *adj.*
plan *n., v.*
plane *n.*
planet *n.*
plant *n., v.*
plastic *n.*
plate *n.*
play *v., n.*
player *n.*
pleasant *adj.*
please *exclamation, v.*
pleased *adj.*
pleasure *n.*
plenty *pron.*
pocket *n.*
poem *n.*
poetry *n.*
point *n., v.*
pointed *adj.*
poison *n., v.*
poisonous *adj.*
police *n.*
polite *adj.*
politely *adv.*
political *adj.*
politician *n.*
politics *n.*
pollution *n.*
pool *n.*
poor *adj.*
popular *adj.*
port *n.*
position *n.*
positive *adj.*
possibility *n.*
possible *adj.*
possibly *adv.*
post *n.*
pot *n.*
potato *n.*
pound *n.*
pour *v.*
powder *n.*
power *n.*
powerful *adj.*
practical *adj.*
practice *n., v.*
prayer *n.*
prefer *v.*
pregnant *adj.*

preparation *n.*
prepare *v.*
present *adj., n., v.*
president *n.*
press *n., v.*
pressure *n.*
pretend *v.*
pretty *adv., adj.*
prevent *v.*
previous *adj.*
price *n.*
priest *n.*
principal *n.*
print *v.*
priority *n.*
prison *n.*
prisoner *n.*
private *adj.*
prize *n.*
probable *adj.*
probably *adv.*
problem *n.*
process *n.*
produce *v.*
product *n.*
production *n.*
professional *adj.*
profit *n.*
program *n.*
progress *n.*
project *n.*
promise *v., n.*
pronunciation *n.*
proof *n.*
proper *adj.*
property *n.*
protect *v.*
protection *n.*
protest *n.*
proud *adj.*
prove *v.*
provide *v.*
public *adj., n.*
   publicly *adv.*
publish *v.*
pull *v.*
punish *v.*
punishment *n.*
pure *adj.*
purple *adj., n.*
purpose *n.*
   on purpose
push *v., n.*
put *v.*

Q

quality *n.*
quantity *n.*
quarter *n.*

queen *n.*
question *n., v.*
quick *adj.*
quickly *adv.*
quiet *adj.*
quietly *adv.*
quite *adv.*

R

race *n., v.*
radio *n.*
railroad *n.*
rain *n., v.*
raise *v.*
rare *adj.*
rarely *adv.*
rate *n.*
rather *adv.*
reach *v.*
reaction *n.*
read *v.*
ready *adj.*
real *adj.*
reality *n.*
realize *v.*
really *adv.*
reason *n.*
reasonable *adj.*
receive *v.*
recent *adj.*
recently *adv.*
recognize *v.*
recommend *v.*
record *n., v.*
recover *v.*
red *adj., n.*
reduce *v.*
refer to *v.*
refuse *v.*
region *n.*
regular *adj.*
regularly *adv.*
relation *n.*
relationship *n.*
relax *v.*
relaxed *adj.*
release *v.*
relevant *adj.*
relief *n.*
religion *n.*
religious *adj.*
rely *v.*
remain *v.*
remark *n.*
remember *v.*
remind *v.*
remove *v.*
rent *n., v.*
repair *v., n.*

The Oxford 2000 List of Keywords

repeat *v.*
replace *v.*
reply *n., v.*
report *v., n.*
reporter *n.*
represent *v.*
request *n., v.*
require *v.*
rescue *v.*
research *n., v.*
reservation *n.*
respect *n., v.*
responsibility *n.*
responsible *adj.*
rest *n., v.*
restaurant *n.*
result *n., v.*
return *v., n.*
rice *n.*
rich *adj.*
rid *v.*: get rid of
ride *v., n.*
right *adj., adv., n.*
ring *n., v.*
rise *n., v.*
risk *n., v.*
river *n.*
road *n.*
rob *v.*
rock *n.*
role *n.*
roll *n., v.*
romantic *adj.*
roof *n.*
room *n.*
root *n.*
rope *n.*
rough *adj.*
round *adj.*
route *n.*
row *n.*
royal *adj.*
rub *v.*
rubber *n.*
rude *adj.*
   rudely *adv.*
ruin *v.*
rule *n., v.*
run *v., n.*
rush *v.*

S

sad *adj.*
sadness *n.*
safe *adj.*
safely *adv.*
safety *n.*
sail *v.*
salad *n.*

sale *n.*
salt *n.*
same *adj., pron.*
sand *n.*
satisfaction *n.*
satisfied *adj.*
sauce *n.*
save *v.*
say *v.*
scale *n.*
scare *v.*
scared *adj.*
scary *adj.*
schedule *n.*
school *n.*
science *n.*
scientific *adj.*
scientist *n.*
scissors *n.*
score *n., v.*
scratch *v., n.*
screen *n.*
search *n., v.*
season *n.*
seat *n.*
second *adj., adv., n.*
secret *adj., n.*
secretary *n.*
secretly *adv.*
section *n.*
see *v.*
seed *n.*
seem *v.*
sell *v.*
send *v.*
senior *adj.*
sense *n.*
sensible *adj.*
sensitive *adj.*
sentence n.
separate *adj., v.*
separately *adv.*
series *n.*
serious *adj.*
serve *v.*
service *n.*
set *n., v.*
settle *v.*
several *adj., pron.*
sew *v.*
sex *n.*
sexual *adj.*
shade *n.*
shadow *n.*
shake *v.*
shame *n.*
shape *n., v.*
   shaped *adj.*
share *v., n.*

sharp *adj.*
she *pron.*
sheep *n.*
sheet *n.*
shelf *n.*
shell *n.*
shine *v.*
shiny *adj.*
ship *n.*
shirt *n.*
shock *n., v.*
shoe *n.*
shoot *v.*
shop *v.*
shopping *n.*
short *adj.*
shot *n.*
should *modal v.*
shoulder *n.*
shout *v., n.*
show *v., n.*
shower *n.*
shut *v.*
shy *adj.*
sick *adj.*
side *n.*
sight *n.*
sign *n., v.*
signal *n.*
silence *n.*
silly *adj.*
silver *n., adj.*
similar *adj.*
simple *adj.*
since *prep., conj., adv.*
sing *v.*
singer *n.*
single *adj.*
sink *v.*
sir *n.*
sister *n.*
sit *v.*
situation *n.*
size *n.*
skill *n.*
skin *n.*
skirt *n.*
sky *n.*
sleep *v., n.*
sleeve *n.*
slice *n.*
slide *v.*
slightly *adv.*
slip *v.*
slow *adj.*
slowly *adv.*
small *adj.*
smell *v., n.*
smile *v., n.*

smoke *n., v.*
smooth *adj.*
   smoothly *adv.*
snake *n.*
snow *n., v.*
so *adv., conj.*
soap *n.*
social *adj.*
society *n.*
sock *n.*
soft *adj.*
soil *n.*
soldier *n.*
solid *adj., n.*
solution *n.*
solve *v.*
some *adj., pron.*
somebody *pron.*
somehow *adv.*
someone *pron.*
something *pron.*
sometimes *adv.*
somewhere *adv.*
son *n.*
song *n.*
soon *adv.*
   as soon as
sore *adj.*
sorry *adj.*
sort *n., v.*
sound *n., v.*
soup *n.*
south *n., adj., adv.*
southern *adj.*
space *n.*
speak *v.*
speaker *n.*
special *adj.*
speech *n.*
speed *n.*
spell *v.*
spend *v.*
spice *n.*
spider *n.*
spirit *n.*
spoil *v.*
spoon *n.*
sport *n.*
spot *n.*
spread *v.*
spring *n.*
square *adj., n.*
stage *n.*
stair *n.*
stamp *n.*
stand *v., n.*
standard *n., adj.*
star *n.*
stare *v.*

start *v., n.*
state *n., v.*
statement *n.*
station *n.*
stay *v.*
steady *adj.*
steal *v.*
steam *n.*
step *n., v.*
stick *v., n.*
sticky *adj.*
still *adv., adj.*
stomach *n.*
stone *n.*
stop *v., n.*
store *n., v.*
storm *n.*
story *n.*
stove *n.*
straight *adv., adj.*
strange *adj.*
street *n.*
strength *n.*
stress *n.*
stretch *v.*
strict *adj.*
string *n.*
strong *adj.*
strongly *adv.*
structure *n.*
struggle *v., n.*
student *n.*
study *n., v.*
stuff *n.*
stupid *adj.*
style *n.*
subject *n.*
substance *n.*
succeed *v.*
success *n.*
successful *adj.*
successfully *adv.*
such *adj.*
   such as
suck *v.*
sudden *adj.*
suddenly *adv.*
suffer *v.*
sugar *n.*
suggest *v.*
suggestion *n.*
suit *n.*
suitable *adj.*
sum *n.*
summer *n.*
sun *n.*
supply *n.*
support *n., v.*
suppose *v.*

sure *adj., adv.*
surface *n.*
surprise *n., v.*
surprised *adj.*
surround *v.*
survive *v.*
swallow *v.*
swear *v.*
sweat *n., v.*
sweet *adj.*
swim *v.*
switch *n., v.*
symbol *n.*
system *n.*

T

table *n.*
tail *n.*
take *v.*
talk *v., n.*
tall *adj.*
tape *n.*
task *n.*
taste *n., v.*
tax *n.*
tea *n.*
teach *v.*
teacher *n.*
team *n.*
tear /tɛr/ *v.*
tear /tɪr/ *n.*
technical *adj.*
technology *n.*
telephone *n.*
television *n.*
tell *v.*
temperature *n.*
temporary *adj.*
tend *v.*
terrible *adj.*
test *n., v.*
text *n.*
than *prep., conj.*
thank *v.*
thanks *n.*
thank you *n.*
that *adj., pron., conj.*
the *definite article*
theater *n.*
their *adj.*
theirs *pron.*
them *pron.*
themselves *pron.*
then *adv.*
there *adv.*
therefore *adv.*
they *pron.*
thick *adj.*
thin *adj.*

thing *n.*
think *v.*
thirsty *adj.*
this *adj., pron.*
though *conj., adv.*
thought *n.*
thread *n.*
threat *n.*
threaten *v.*
throat *n.*
through *prep., adv.*
throw *v.*
thumb *n.*
ticket *n.*
tie *v., n.*
tight *adj., adv.*
time *n.*
tire *n.*
tired *adj.*
title *n.*
to *prep., infinitive marker*
today *adv., n.*
toe *n.*
together *adv.*
toilet *n.*
tomato *n.*
tomorrow *adv., n.*
tongue *n.*
tonight *adv., n.*
too *adv.*
tool *n.*
tooth *n.*
top *n., adj.*
topic *n.*
total *adj., n.*
totally *adv.*
touch *v., n.*
tour *n.*
tourist *n.*
toward *prep.*
towel *n.*
town *n.*
toy *n.*
track *n.*
tradition *n.*
traffic *n.*
train *n., v.*
training *n.*
translate *v.*
transparent *adj.*
transportation *n.*
trash *n.*
travel *v., n.*
treat *v.*
treatment *n.*
tree *n.*
trial *n.*
trick *n.*
trip *n., v.*

trouble *n.*
truck *n.*
true *adj.*
trust *n., v.*
truth *n.*
try *v.*
tube *n.*
tune *n.*
tunnel *n.*
turn *v., n.*
TV *n.*
twice *adv.*
twist *v.*
type *n., v.*
typical *adj.*

U

ugly *adj.*
unable *adj.*
uncle *n.*
uncomfortable *adj.*
unconscious *adj.*
under *prep., adv.*
underground *adj., adv.*
understand *v.*
underwater *adj., adv.*
underwear *n.*
unemployment *n.*
unexpected *adj.*
unexpectedly *adv.*
unfair *adj.*
unfortunately *adv.*
unfriendly *adj.*
unhappy *adj.*
uniform *n.*
union *n.*
unit *n.*
universe *n.*
university *n.*
unkind *adj.*
unknown *adj.*
unless *conj.*
unlikely *adj.*
unlucky *adj.*
unpleasant *adj.*
until *conj., prep.*
unusual *adj.*
up *adv., prep.*
upper *adj.*
upset *v., adj.*
upstairs *adv., adj.*
upward *adv.*
urgent *adj.*
us *pron.*
use *v., n.*
used *adj.*
used to *modal v.*
useful *adj.*
user *n.*

The Oxford 2000 List of Keywords

usual *adj.*
usually *adv.*

V

vacation *n.*
valley *n.*
valuable *adj.*
value *n.*
variety *n.*
various *adj.*
vary *v.*
vegetable *n.*
vehicle *n.*
very *adv.*
video *n.*
view *n.*
violence *n.*
violent *adj.*
virtually *adv.*
visit *v., n.*
visitor *n.*
voice *n.*
volume *n.*
vote *n., v.*

W

wait *v.*
wake (up) *v.*
walk *v., n.*
wall *n.*
want *v.*
war *n.*
warm *adj., v.*
warn *v.*
wash *v.*
waste *v., n., adj.*
watch *v., n.*
water *n.*
wave *n., v.*
way *n.*
we *pron.*
weak *adj.*
weakness *n.*
weapon *n.*
wear *v.*
weather *n.*
website *n.*
wedding *n.*
week *n.*
weekend *n.*
weigh *v.*
weight *n.*
welcome *v.*
well *adv., adj., exclamation*
　　as well (as)
west *n., adj., adv.*
western *adj.*
wet *adj.*
what *pron., adj.*

whatever *adj., pron., adv.*
wheel *n.*
when *adv., conj.*
whenever *conj.*
where *adv., conj.*
wherever *conj.*
whether *conj.*
which *pron., adj.*
while *conj., n.*
white *adj., n.*
who *pron.*
whoever *pron.*
whole *adj., n.*
whose *adj., pron.*
why *adv.*
wide *adj.*
wife *n.*
wild *adj.*
will *modal v., n.*
win *v.*
wind /wɪnd/ *n.*
window *n.*
wine *n.*
wing *n.*
winner *n.*
winter *n.*
wire *n.*
wish *v., n.*
with *prep.*
within *prep.*
without *prep.*
woman *n.*
wonder *v.*
wonderful *adj.*
wood *n.*
wooden *adj.*
wool *n.*
word *n.*
work *v., n.*
worker *n.*
world *n.*
worried *adj.*
worry *v.*
worse *adj., adv.*
worst *adj., adv., n.*
worth *adj.*
would *modal v.*
wrap *v.*
wrist *n.*
write *v.*
writer *n.*
writing *n.*
wrong *adj., adv.*

Y

yard *n.*
year *n.*
yellow *adj., n.*
yes *exclamation*

yesterday *adv., n.*
yet *adv.*
you *pron.*
young *adj.*
your *adj.*
yours *pron.*
yourself *pron.*
youth *n.*